The
Message
Delivered

"You know that I kept back nothing that was for your good: I delivered the message to you; I taught you in public and in your homes. . . ."   Acts 20:20

The

Message

Delivered

C. S. MANN

MOREHOUSE-BARLOW CO.

NEW YORK

© 1973 Morehouse-Barlow Co.
14 East 41st Street, New York, N. Y. 10017

SBN 0-8192-1143-5

Library of Congress Catalog Card No. 73-84097

Printed in the United States of America

*To the Sisters of the Community of
the Holy Rood, Middlesbrough, England
with affection and deep gratitude*

PREFACE

For all the fact that Paul's letters are extensively read in church, the gigantic stature of Paul as traveler, thinker, and man of action does not really strike us unless we take the trouble to make a patient journey through the Acts of the Apostles. Even then, we are likely to miss the real perils which travel carried with in in the days when Paul was exercising his vocation to teach the Gospel.

This book is an attempt to provide some background to the journeys and the hazards which accompanied them. And, yet, Paul the Apostle without the Jerusalem church is really unthinkable, however much he may have thought that his fellows—Jewish Christians in Jerusalem—were mistaken in their emphasis on their "Jewishness." Perhaps, therefore, the somewhat abrupt transition from Peter to Paul in Acts was deliberate on Luke's part. The universality of sin demanded universal remedy, as Paul clearly saw, and Judaism, however precious, could not long have remained a vehicle for Paul's tempestuous preaching and teaching ministry.

My thanks are due to Miss Mary Moore for her great forbearance and patience in typing the original manuscript from recorded tapes and to Mrs. Helen Thomsen, author of the *Leader's Guide*, for her customary, exemplary patience with the author. The dedication bears witness to a shared bond of more than twenty-five years.

C. S. Mann

CONTENTS

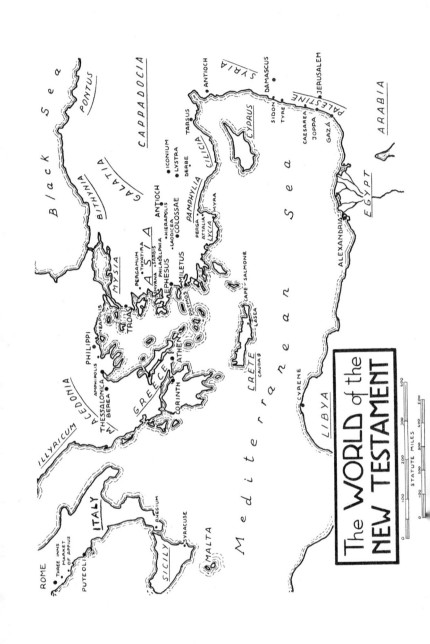

The WORLD of the NEW TESTAMENT

STATUTE MILES

1. AN EARLY LOTTERY
(Acts I)

IT IS of considerable importance for anyone who wishes to study the Acts of the Apostles to achieve some sense of proportion about the numbers of people involved initially in the early Christian community and about the way in which official Judaism regarded this new religious loyalty. Our difficulty is that, when we pick up the Acts of the Apostles, we are confronted with a document written from the standpoint of the early Christian community itself. We are being asked to look at the reactions first of Judaism and later of Roman imperial authority through the eyes of one for whom the events of these early years were of tremendous importance. If the first part of the Acts of the Apostles had been written by a Jew whose home was in Jerusalem, we would have an entirely different perspective on the early history of the Christian Church. From the point of view of the Roman imperial authority it would be even more difficult—supposing we were reading the Acts of the Apostles as a pagan Roman citizen—to achieve any sense of balance between the claims of this small Christian community on the one hand and those of the vastly more numerous Jewish body on the other. Yet, it is important that we make the attempt before we try to see what lies behind the recollections and the records which are contained in the Acts of the Apostles.

Traditionally—and there seems very little reason to deny the core of the tradition—the book called Acts was written by Luke, who was also the author of the gospel which comes third in the four gospels in the New Testament. Unfortunately, there seem to be hundreds of conflicting opinions on the part of New Testament

1

scholars as to why Luke wrote this work. While it seems
certain from the preface that he intended it to be a kind
of sequel to the gospel which bears his name, the book
itself does not provide us with a sufficient number of
firm indications as to what exact purpose he might have
had in mind. It would have been of help, for example,
to have had some information about the "Theophilus"
to whom he addresses this book. Unhappily, we do not
know whether Theophilus was a pagan, someone acquainted with the synagogue worship of Judaism, or a
"Godfearer"[1] who was attempting to make up his mind
about the claims of this new community which we now
know as the Church.

Some scholars have suggested, for example, that Luke
wrote Acts as an *"apologia"*[2] to an interested Roman
official—or even to more than one—in order to prove
that Christianity grew out of Judaism and as such was a
religion to be officially "tolerated" under Roman law.
Others have suggested that Luke wrote it as an account
of the life and ministry of Paul as a Christian. This
particular explanation does not seem to be very convincing. The first part of Acts is entirely concerned with
the infant Church in Jerusalem and Paul, while he is
first referred to in Acts 7, does not emerge really as an
important figure until later chapters of the book. The
early chapters are almost entirely concerned with events
in and around Jerusalem. Even when attention and
interest shifts to Paul there is still a considerable amount
of time devoted to Paul's relations with Jerusalem, both
on the religious and on the civic level.

Within fairly recent years, the suggestion has been
made that Luke wrote his work in order to answer the
questionings and doubts of those who had been led to
expect an early return of Jesus, as Messiah, in glory to
the scene of his former ministry and were puzzled to
know why this had not taken place. This suggestion

usually goes on to assert that Luke wrote his second book in order to prove that Jesus had intended all along that there should be a continuing Messianic Community and that any expectation of return, or of the "End," must, inevitably, be long delayed.

In any event, the purpose of Luke in writing Acts is not made any more open to our inspection by the fact that the book ends almost abruptly with the imprisonment of Paul in Rome, leaving us with a multitude of unanswered questions. Even the great hero of the earlier chapters of Acts—the apostle Peter—appears to vanish from the scene at an early stage in the "Jerusalem" part of the book, being referred to only once or twice after that. It seems best—for the purposes of this book—to set such questions aside and concentrate, instead, on seeing what the book can tell us about the life and beliefs of the early Christian community.

The book opens on a rather puzzling note. It begins, after the statement of its purpose, with an account of the last appearance of Jesus to the inner circle of those who followed him through his ministry. The account is puzzling for several reasons. In the first place, it reads as though there was a period of forty days between the time Jesus was raised from the dead and his return to the Father. In the second place, there are striking similarities in the language between Luke's account of the transfiguration,[3] his account of Jesus' resurrection,[4] and the account in Acts of this last appearance of Jesus to his disciples. If you put the three accounts side by side you will soon see this. But perhaps the most puzzling thing of all is the suggestion apparent in Luke's words that after his resurrection Jesus belonged neither to heaven nor to earth and that it was only on the occasion (which Christians have for many centuries called the "ascension") that Jesus finally came to share once again the glory of the Father. That this cannot really be so, we see when we look at the stories of the resurrection of Jesus as they appear in the Gospels. In the first chapter of Acts is a *theologizing* of Jesus' last appearance to those who were intimate with him in his life and ministry and who were with him within a very short time of his resurrection.

There is no doubt, judging from the records of the gospels, that those who were with Jesus during the appearances after his resurrection were themselves considerably puzzled by the experiences. The attempts made, for example, by Luke[5] and John[6] to explain the physical appearance of Jesus in those post-resurrection manifestations are evidence of the bewilderment felt by those who had known Jesus in the days of his ministry. This is understandable, since resurrection—in the way in which this applies to Jesus in our gospels—was entirely beyond the realm of human experience. It ought, therefore, to be of no surprise to us that the last appearance of Jesus after his resurrection would occasion doubt and hesitation. Would Jesus appear yet another time? To what extent had the ministry which they had known really ended? How is it possible to accommodate these post-resurrection appearances to the kind of references which Jesus had made during his ministry to a continuing community of disciples? Was it the case that these appearances had come to an end with a finality which left a great deal unexplained?

We fall too easily into the trap of looking at the first years of the infant Church through the eyes of the kind of statements which are made in the classical creeds of Christendom—the so-called Apostles' Creed and the creed of the Council of Nicaea. We forget that the statements made in the Creeds about the nature of God himself, of the ministry of Jesus, and of the continuing work of the Holy Spirit in the community are the result of long reflection and often bitter debate. If we expect to find neat theological packages and well rounded credal statements in the New Testament—especially in the Acts of the Apostles—we shall not only be asking the wrong questions, we shall, in most cases, be looking in vain.

Here, then, we have a group of men, eleven where once there were twelve, faced with a phenomenon (the resurrection) which in spite of the promises of Jesus was wholly outside experience and possibly completely beyond expectation. The bewilderment, we can only guess at; the reactions to the phenomenon, we can glimpse beneath the surface of the records. What Luke has provided for us in the first chapter of the Acts of the Apostles is a dramatization of Jesus' last appearance to his disciples, an appearance which left many, many questions unanswered and the disciples with the responsibility of reflecting upon the events they had witnessed, the words which they had heard, the teaching they had received, and of making their own responses to the questions thus raised.

From the time of the last appearance of Jesus to the nucleus of the infant community, the old pattern of ministry and physical presence was over forever. It is in light of this fact, slowly digested and reflected upon, that we must see and evaluate the importance of the preservation (especially by John) of the recollected words of Jesus about the continued presence of the Holy Spirit within the community.[7] It is not surprising that one of the classical phrases in early Christian liturgy was the expression "the Holy Spirit in the Holy Church." Luke presents a picture of the inner heart and core of the future community, eleven men together with a number of people associated with them, facing the future, uncertain as to whether the physical manifestation of Jesus had ended forever. He presents, too, a picture of the infant community going back into the framework of the life of their own Judaism.

It is at this point that we must exercise a sense of proportion about the beginning chapters of the Acts of the Apostles. It is clear from these early chapters that the first Christians still regarded themselves as being practicing Jews. It is also clear, from these same chapters of Acts, that the authorities of orthodox Judaism in Jerusalem regarded these early Christians as Jews and judged them as such. It is true that orthodox Judaism in Jerusalem considered the members of the new community—which acknowledged Jesus as the promised Messiah—as being a somewhat troublesome sect. This would not have occasioned much more than irritated questioning on the part of official Judaism. There had been messianic claimants before and there would, no doubt, be many more in the future. The followers of former claimants to Messiahship had managed to remain more or less within the rather loose boundaries of Judaism. Judaism[8] had more than a little experience of sectarian activity both within and on the fringes of its own life. To this extent, therefore, the early Christian community depicted for us in Acts would have been regarded by official Judaism as possessing no more than "nuisance value."

The election of someone to take the place of the traitor Judas in the company of "the twelve," is described for us by Luke in the first chapter of Acts. Here—as in the gospels—we find Peter acting as spokesman for this inner group. There are many reasons which might be given for the stabilization of the inner circle around the number twelve, the one coming most easily to mind being identification of the twelve with the twelve tribes of ancient Israel. This identification, as a matter of fact, is found in many places in the New Testament and has an honored place in the last book in the New Testament collection.[9] It is likely that during the ministry of Jesus the actual number of those who were closest to Jesus

may have varied and it is more than likely that an
exclusive number of twelve was arrived at finally only
in apostolic times.

Within recent years another interesting suggestion has
been made. This is that the organization of the Jerusalem
Church was modeled very largely on that of the Essene
community at Qumran. There was, most assuredly, an
inner council of twelve at Qumran, and this, it is almost
certain, reflected the somewhat self-conscious exclusive
identification of the Essenes themselves with a "true
Israel." This is not the only factor to be taken into account
when we think of the organization of the Jerusalem
church. We know from the gospels that within the inner
circle of twelve there was a group of three—Peter, James
and John—who seemed to have been present with Jesus
at all the most vital points of his ministry. Some scholars
say it is highly significant that within the Essene community at Qumran there was also an inner determinative
group of three in whose hands final decision apparently
rested. What we do not know at this moment is
whether or not this Essene inner group of three was
composed of members of the council of twelve. However,
what must be taken seriously in the future, in the light
of the discoveries at Qumran, is the facility with which
the Jerusalem Church organized itself after the resurrection of Jesus. It is possible—as many scholars have
suggested—that the Jerusalem Church deliberately chose
an organizational model near to hand, *i.e.*, the institutions
found at Qumran among the Essenes. It is only fair to
say that much of this kind of thinking is, at best,
speculative, though many scholars are impressed by the
parallels between the Jerusalem Church and the Essene
community.[10]

More important, however, is the election of Mathias
into the collegial body of the apostles. We know nothing
at all of Mathias apart from his name, though it is worth

pointing out that his name is similar to that of Matthew, both in Syriac and in Aramaic. For all we know, Mathias may well have had some part in the compilation of what we now know as Matthew's gospel. It may be that one of the reasons for his being chosen as a possible candidate was his intimate knowledge of the events in the ministry of Jesus. Certainly, this is how Luke represents his candidacy to us in Acts.[11]

There is a common assumption based on our present English versions of the Acts of the Apostles that there was an almost unlimited number of people from whom to choose candidates. This assumption rises from an acceptance at face value of the assertion in Acts 1:22 that a candidate must have been someone who had been present not only through the baptizing ministry of John, but also through the public and private ministry of Jesus. Acts 1:22 almost certainly ought to read (in translation): "There is no one left who accompanied us during all the time that the Lord Jesus went in and out among us, beginning at the baptism of John ..." Therefore, one of the men there had to be chosen in Judas' place as witness to the resurrection (not to the ministry of Jesus).[12]

Incidentally, however odd the practice may appear to be to us, the choosing by lot of a person to fulfill a particularly important and sensitive function was common in the time we are studying and has ample Old Testament precedent. Perhaps, this might give us room for thought when we contemplate the amount of machinery, bureaucratic and otherwise, by which we choose men for the Christian ministry today.

NOTES

1. "Godfearer" was a technical term applied to pagans who were attracted to Judaism, even attending synagogue worship, but who did not commit themselves to conversion to Judaism. For many pagans, the monotheism of Judaism was a factor of im-

mense importance, particularly at the beginning of the Christian era when the old gods had largely lost whatever credibility they had.

2. An *apologia* is best understood as an explanation of a particular line of conduct on the part of an individual, or an explanation of the beliefs and practices of a group. Perhaps the best known illustration of the word is John Henry Cardinal Newman's famous work, *Apologia pro vita sua,* published to explain why Cardinal Newman became a Roman Catholic.

3. Luke 9:28-36   4. Luke 24   5. *Ibid*   6. John 20, 21

7. For example: John 6:63; 7:39; 14:16-17 and 25-26; 15:26; 16:7-15; 20:22-23.

8. C. S. Mann, *The Man for All Time.* New York: Morehouse-Barlow Co., 1971.

9. Revelation 12:1; 21:9-21; 22:2.

10. For a more detailed discussion of this subject, see *The Anchor Bible,* Volume 31, *The Acts of the Apostles,* Johannes Munck. New York: Doubleday & Company, Inc., 1967. There is, also, much useful material in *The Scrolls and the New Testament,* ed. Krister Stendahl. London: SCM Press, 1958.

11. Apart from the importance which Luke evidently attached to the election of a man to take Judas' place in the band of disciples (now apostles), it is possible that Luke was reminding his readers—through this episode which he records at length—of the origins in the community of a man who had some part in the compilation of the Gospel of Matthew.

12. *Cf.* Albright, William F. and C. S. Mann, *St. Matthew,* Anchor Bible. New York: Doubleday & Company, Inc., 1972, pp. CLXXIII-IV.

2. DESCRIPTION OF AN INDESCRIBABLE EXPERIENCE

(Acts 2:1-13)

WE NOW pass on to what, for Luke, was the definitive event in the life of the early Christian community—the experience of enabling power described for us in his second chapter. It is important to try to evaluate the kind of descriptive language which Luke is using since it is possible to emerge from a reading of it with quite erroneous ideas.

First, let's remember that the feast of Pentecost was (and still is in Judaism) an important festival. Aside from its agricultural origins in the law of Moses,[1] it had by New Testament times achieved a whole range of meanings and interpretations which are important to any understanding of Luke's work: It commemorated the giving of the Law on Mount Sinai—for the Jew, not only the badge of his own distinctiveness but also the badge of freedom under Law. It looked, as did the harvest around which in agricultural days it revolved, to judgment and the ingathering at the end of time. And, among the Essenes, it had taken on a new importance in being preeminently a feast of a New Covenant.

With the last of these meanings, it is worth spending a little time. We know of the tremendous importance of the phrase "New Covenant" in the gospels.[2] That expression is also of vital importance in the first letter of Paul to Corinth and in the book which we call the epistle to the Hebrews. We ought not to be surprised, therefore, to find that, for the first Christians approaching the feast of Pentecost, the implications of the festival with its emphasis on New Covenant were a matter of tremendous importance and even excitement.

When we come to ask ourselves the question: "What happened on that first Christian Pentecost?" we are likely to find ourselves in the middle of conflicting interpretations and possible understandings of the event. To begin with, it was assumed, through many centuries of Christian history, that there was such an outpouring of the empowering majesty of the Holy Spirit that those who were gathered in the upstairs room in Jerusalem began to speak in foreign languages. In fact, this seems to be the interpretation favored by the English translation of the Jerusalem Bible. The author finds it extremely difficult to understand how this interpretation can survive the sober light of investigation. It is clearly stated by Luke that all the men who witnessed the event—or rather, who heard the explanations of the event by the apostles— were Jews.[3] Here were Jews, gathered from every part of the Mediterranean world for a specifically Jewish festival whose origin and purpose they knew, and of whose interpretation they were well aware. We are asked to suppose that they were stupefied by a group of men speaking in the languages of their own countries of residence. Since synagogue worship in all parts of the Mediterranean was carried on—so far as the reading of scripture and the prayers were concerned—in Hebrew and/or Aramaic, it is a little hard to understand just what function would have been served by a miraculous out- pouring of speeches in foreign languages.

There is an interpretation of this phenomenon which is far more widely accepted today among New Testament scholars, and that is that the apostles were speaking under great spiritual and emotional stress in what has come to be called "glossolalia." Certainly it is true in the light of the accusations made against the Apostles (that they were drunk—Acts 2:15) that this kind of manifestation of intense spiritual and emotional excitement fits the story much better as we have it, than any explanation about foreign languages. The phenomenon of "glossolalia"— speaking, uttering, singing, whether accompanied by physical movement or not, in sounds outside the experi- ence of ordinary articulation—has occurred all through pagan, Jewish, and Christian history. It is supposed by Old Testament scholars that many of the prophets attached to local shrines in the days of ancient Israel were accustomed very often to authenticate their pro- nouncements by ecstatic utterances. There is nothing particularly Christian, and certainly nothing particularly

Jewish, about this phenomenon. It is one which, for centuries, has been deliberately drug induced among some Indian tribes in the United States.

Having said that, it may be well at this point to pay some attention to *glossolalia* as it presently exists in most denominations in the United States and elsewhere. First, many of the claims—theological and otherwise—made on behalf of the phenomenon by some of its advocates are often misplaced and in some cases misleading. It is not true, for example, that the proclamations of John the Baptist and Jesus spoke of a "baptism of the spirit" as though this was in some way separate and distinct from the baptism in water and the baptism of judgment. Any competent New Testament scholar is aware that the phraseology of Mark 1:8 and Matthew 3:11, for example, is a parallelism which is found in the Essene literature of Qumran.[4] Secondly, there are grave reasons for holding as suspect any claims that such conduct is *necessarily* inspired by the Holy Spirit. The apostle Paul—even though he himself spoke in "tongues"—found himself compelled to utter strong warnings against any who place final reliance on such a phenomenon.[5] This apostolic testimony and warning has been echoed down through Christian history, and the consensus of warning has been very nearly universal. One of the greatest of all authorities on the spiritual and ascetic life, St. Teresa of Avila, was particularly outspoken—even vehement—in her condemnation of the use of ecstasy as a yardstick of spiritual benediction. Thirdly, it is to be hoped that those who find themselves attracted, or puzzled, by the phenomenon of *glossolalia* will some time take the trouble to read Dr. William Sargant's perceptive study, *The Battle for the Mind*.[6] Lastly, the author of this book finds himself wondering what kind of Christian practice is left to fall back on when those who have relied heavily upon this type of spiritual experience find themselves, as we all do for long periods of time, bereft of any sense of the presence of God. It is certainly not without significance that the attitude of total dependence of an initiate into this kind of practice upon the one who introduced him or her to it was noticed by Dr. Sargant and other experts in the mental processes. It is a dependence which may well produce a rebirth or a new outbreak of spiritual adolescence, in which the believer feels the compulsion to "go along" with current patterns at one time, while at another, strives to break loose into an identity of his own. It is one of the disturbing features of some kinds of "Pentecostalism" that those who cannot, or do not, share its practices and presuppositions are sometimes regarded as less "spiritual" or less "converted" than those who share the experience.[7]

After all that has been said, it is still true that emotion which is rigidly suppressed, or for long periods of time totally inhibited, has a habit of breaking out in somewhat unpleasant directions. The reader is referred again to Dr. William Sargant's very good analysis of the subject. Many of us find it possible to give full rein to emotion and spiritual uplift through the liturgical and semi-liturgical worship which is the Church's constant diet of prayer. Perhaps the upsurge of interest in what is called "Pentecostalism" in our own time has something to say about the arid way in which we have approached the staple diet of worship—that is, the scriptures and common prayer—as well as something to say about our own grasp of the realities of our pilgrimage to God.

There are, then, puzzling features about the account of what happened at that first Christian Pentecost. The interpretation I propose to offer here is one which has been explored in other places; all I can attempt to do is to summarize what has been said on previous occasions. To begin with, let us notice, as we pointed out earlier, that the men to whom Peter spoke after the great outburst of excitement were Jews. What has been suggested by me elsewhere, and what I am suggesting now, is that Peter and his companions were offering a totally new explanation of the feast of Pentecost, not only in the light of their own experience of the empowering glory of the Holy Spirit, but also offering their explanations of Pentecost in terms of the customary liturgical lessons for the feast itself. Once again, it would be unfair to the reader to go into lengthy explanations of the Greek text of the story of the first Pentecost as we now have it, and I apologize to the reader for asserting quite bluntly that the Greek of Acts 2:8 and 2:11 can—and in my view does—bear very well the interpretation that the apostles were explaining—to everyone's intense astonishment—the feast of Pentecost in the light of the establishment of a new covenant of salvation. It would be hardly surprising for the crowd who heard this astonishing assertion to have concluded that the speakers were all drunk.

It is evident that something out of the ordinary happened at that first Christian Pentecost, but it is very difficult to determine just what it was that did happen. At any rate, Pentecost was seen by the author of Acts to be the decisive point from which the early Christian community began to be conscious of itself as the people of a new covenant. My own views on the modern preoccupation with signs of the Spirit—whether true or false—have already been given. We shall discover, not only in the Acts but also in the letters of Paul, that the preoccupation of the early Christians with "signs" or marks of the Spirit was a very decided factor in early Christian history.

NOTES

1. Exodus 34:22
   Leviticus 23:15-22
   Deuteronomy 16:9-10

2. See *The Man for All Time,* Mann, pp. 16-17, 92, 104-6, for further study of this point.
3. Acts 2:5. Some texts read "devout men" rather than "devout Jews."
4. *Cf.* Matthew 3:7-12; Luke 3:7-17; Mark 1:4, 7, 8 with the Qumran *Rule of the Community,* ii: 8; 4, 13; *Hymns of Thanksgiving* vi: 18; *Habakkuk Commentary* ii:11-13; *Damascus Document* ii:5, 6. It is one of the Thanksgiving Psalms of the Essenes which speaks most clearly of the "river of fire" as a synonym for judgment.
5. I Corinthians 14
6. Penguin, 1961. Along with Dr. Sargant's book, the interested reader might read R. A. Knox's *Enthusiasm,* Oxford University Press, which deals at length with the very varied history of the many "Charismatic" groups throughout Christian history. Sargant is concerned with phenomena which characterize too close a dependence on a felt, "enthusiastic," response, whether that response is to the Gospel, or to a political ideology. There are, the author maintains, very real psychological parallels between "brainwashing" and the contagious nature of worship which is too often channeled into noisy expressions of fervor. Another book to be looked into on this subject is William Samarin, *Tongues of Men and Angels: The Religious Language of Pentacostalism.* New York: The Macmillan Company, 1972.
7. It must be emphasized that the opinions expressed here are those of the author. His own reservations may be summarized as springing from his doubts as to whether God does repeat himself in history so as to reproduce in our time the phenomena associated with the early Christian community. He also finds it difficult to accept as "charismatic renewal" an implied rejection of other charisms such as administration which Paul certainly accounted to be one of the gifts of the spirit.

3. THE FIRST LONG SERMON

(Acts 2:14-47)

PETER'S SPEECH to the crowd at that first Pentecost contains the first statement by the leader of the apostles about the significance they had learned to attach to Jesus. Incidentally, since we have no information about the scriptural lessons read in synagogue worship or in the temple at the feast of Pentecost in New Testament times, we don't know whether the quotation from Joel[1] with which Peter is represented as beginning was one of the prescribed lessons for Pentecost. What is important in Peter's speech is the theological content which he, in his own words, gives to the life and ministry of Jesus. There is a recognizable pattern in these early speeches in Acts, a pattern which led a prominent British New Testament scholar, Dr. C. H. Dodd,[2] to attach to them the description "the apostolic preaching." The Greek word—which has passed into the technical New Testament vocabulary—is *kerygma*. The word itself means the kind of proclamation made by a herald in ancient times. Dr. Dodd's book exercised a very wide influence on New Testament scholarship in its own time and the interested reader would certainly gain a good deal by studying it. While it is true that New Testament scholarship today is not as impressed by Dodd's remarks as were scholars when the book was first published, it is worthwhile detailing here the analysis which Dodd made of the speeches in the early part of Acts. He maintains that, with some slight variation, all the speeches have a common pattern and a common theory of themes. Here they are:

1. All things to which the apostles gave witness were events which had been fulfilled from the scriptures of the Old Testament. All the early history of God's ancient people was summed up and reached its peak in the mission of John the Baptist.
2. God declared himself supremely and definitively by his acts of salvation in the ministry of Jesus, reaching a climax of God's revealing of himself in Jesus in the passion and resurrection.
3. The witness of the apostles, and those who were testifying to these things, supported all this testimony as true.

4. Jesus is both Lord and Messiah and he is in glory at "the right hand of God"; it is he who gives the Holy Spirit. The raising of Jesus from death by God is the final proof of the Messiahship and the glory of Jesus. The Holy Spirit is at one and the same time the guarantee and the first installment of the gifts of the New Age.

5. There is, therefore, an obligation on the part of all men who hear this message and respond to it to repent and be baptized.

From time to time New Testament scholars have cast some doubt upon the authenticity and the historical truth of these speeches—or sermons, as we may prefer to call them—as they are reported by Luke in Acts. It is said, for example, that these speeches bear all the marks of having been written by the author of Acts along the lines of what he supposed the early Christian teachers and preachers must have said. It has also been suggested that these speeches are so formal and stylized that a serious element of doubt is introduced as to why Luke did not record the apostles drawing upon their own reminiscences of the ministry of Jesus. Criticisms vary from one New Testament scholar to another, but, generally speaking, those two objections summarize the burden of most of the criticism over the course of the last thirty years or more.

It is possible that the critics who suggest that Luke was deliberately composing pieces of material along the lines of what he thought the apostles must have said or ought to have said failed to take into account one very important point. We are now in a far better position today than we were twenty years ago, to appreciate and understand the technicalities and the techniques of rabbinic tradition as it was taught and handed down from one Jewish teacher to another and from a Jewish teacher to his pupils. We know now, for example, that teaching by the rabbis tended to formalize very quickly into fixed patterns so that it could be remembered easily. Indeed, it is possible that a great deal of the similarities in our first three gospels in the way in which they present the teaching of Jesus owes far more to the way in which Jesus taught than to any extensive borrowing of material between one gospel writer and another.

Two other considerations should be mentioned here. The first is that when we come to the teaching of Paul, and his proclamation of the ministry and message of Jesus, in Acts 13:17-41, we find Paul using exactly the same kind of framework as that detailed above. Paul had been taught—as he tells us himself—by the celebrated Rabbi Gamaliel, and his speech in Acts 13 bears exactly the same marks of formality and style of structure as that to be found in the early chapters of Acts. In the second place, these speeches or sermons were addressed to Jews. It is extremely difficult to see how any kind of appeal could have been made to Jews about the ministry of Jesus and its significance without the kind of background appeal to the Old Testament scriptures we find in these early addresses of the Apostles.

The broad lines of any appeal by the apostles to their fellow Jews had been laid down on this first occasion of public preaching. It is interesting to notice that we have here the beginnings of what we now call theology—that is to say the attempt to give expression in human words and interpretation of those acts of salvation by which God in Jesus gave man an access to himself in total freedom. If you look at Peter's first speech in Acts 2, especially verse 36, you will see that there is here an absolute assertion by Peter that Jesus was "made" Lord and Messiah through his being raised from the dead by the Father. Yet, if we compare this with another address by Peter to another gathering of his fellow Jews in the following chapter (Acts 3:12-26), we can observe a shift in Peter's thinking. In that later

chapter (verse 20) Peter seems to imply that the
Messiah has not yet come. Peter has no doubt as to *who*
the Messiah will be—it will be Jesus—yet the whole drift
of the concluding part of this address of Peter seems to
say that Jesus in his ministry and work was, so to speak,
his own Forerunner. This, of course, strikes us as being
completely contradictory. Yet we would be guilty of the
gravest kind of mistake if we supposed that the whole
understanding of Christian faith was—like a later dream
of Peter[3]—let down from heaven ready-made in a neat
package deal. On the contrary, we find all kinds of
hesitations, deliberations, and questionings as to the
interpretation of God's act in Jesus in the New Testament.
The later formulations of the Apostles Creed or the
Nicene Creed and the later Church councils were an
attempt to deal faithfully with the New Testament
evidence.

Much of the teaching of Jesus laid down broad
principles, but there is very little indication that Jesus
made any attempt to spell out in detail how the
principles were to be applied. To use one example, the
attitude of the New Testament writers to the burning
question of the duty of the individual Christian—or of
the whole Christian Church—to the secular state can
frequently be set in parallel contradictory columns. The
apostle Paul varies his attitude from one letter to another,
while the book of Revelation cannot see the Roman
imperial authority as being anything but a sordid and
discredited instrument of repression and persecution. This
particular question has plagued Christians ever since
New Testament times; it is certainly not resolved to this
day.

Or, to use another example, there very soon emerged
a question which was only partially resolved by the
ministry of Paul. That was the attitude of the Jewish
Christians towards those who came to baptism from a

pagan background. We ought not, therefore, to expect ready-made and easy solutions to practical problems of Christian living from our New Testament even though there are some absolutes of Christian conduct. Still less ought we to expect that the New Testament writers, attempting to give expression to their faith almost under the shadow of the cross and the resurrection, will necessarily agree always in their interpretations with one another, or even that they will provide us with the kind of philosophical and theological language which finds expression in the Nicene Creed.

Only gradually did theological questions begin to arise in the early Christian community. Obviously, the first question which arose in men's minds could be put in a form such as, "Who was Jesus, and what was the relationship of his Messianic ministry to God?" The conviction of the early Christians about Jesus was that God had acted in a definitive and final way in Jesus. This act of God in Jesus could be summed up in the one word "salvation." Yet, both the question and the word raise a whole universe of further questions and a further universe of words to explain the single word "salvation." Granted, for example, that God had acted in Jesus, granted that Jesus spoke of himself (at any rate according to John)[4] as Messiah, it was nevertheless the case that there was an almost limitless number of viewpoints which went into the making up of what Christians call "the Messianic expectation." And, if Jesus was a savior-figure, to what extent did the salvation he offered fulfill the aspirations of the Judaism of his own time, or did that salvation look to something deeper and include all men within its scope? These are the kinds of questions which led ultimately to the formulation of the decrees and the statements of later Church councils. The Jerusalem Church as we see it in the Acts of the Apostles was concerned to proclaim the massive truth that God had decisively intervened in the field of human history, within the confines of Judaism, and had, moreover, done so at an identifiable point in human history when Pontius Pilate was procurator of Judaea and Annas and Caiaphas were high priests. We shall meet with this kind of theological question as we go along, especially when we come to the ministry of Paul.

One thing which to the reader seems to characterize the life of the Jerusalem Church in Acts is what may be called, loosely, "enthusiasm." On some levels this enthusiasm seems to us to have been almost unrestrained. Yet, we shall be taking a very superficial view of the infant community if we seek to explain its life and its institutions solely in terms of enthusiasm. We need to remember in discussing the Jerusalem Church that it was composed of Jews who were certainly not given to building a whole life style simply on enthusiasm. Unexamined and unrestrained enthusiasm leads in the end to nothing but unsought trouble. If some Christians were unaware of this basic truth at their conversion, it needs to be added, they very soon learned!

An interesting insight into the early Christian community comes in the second chapter of Acts in a short section of verses 42-47. The faithfulness of the community to apostolic teaching is exercised alongside a faithfulness of the community to the practice of temple-worship. Apparently, they felt—in confessing Jesus as Messiah—no inconsistency in continuing to frequent the temple, even daily. It is not clear whether the phrase "the breaking of bread" was or was not a description of the Eucharist. Since the phrase does not appear as a regular title for the Eucharist until very much later, it may be doubted whether anything more is intended at this point than to describe an early Christian practice whereby the Christian communities met together to share a common meal. Other features of the life as described in this short section seem to indicate a communistic society, complete with common property and a shared responsibility for financial resources. Those who look back with nostalgia upon such a life-style, seeking to find in it a panacea for all the ills of the Christian Church at this present time, should ask themselves how far they suppose such a life-style is possible in anything more than very small, well defined "family" groups. The author finds it difficult to understand how the Christian Church could have spread or even survived had it continued to operate at that level.

NOTES

1. Verses 17-21 (Joel 2:28-32)   2. *Apostolic Preaching*, Harper Row, 1939.   3. Acts 10:9-16   4. John 4:25-26

4. A CHRISTIAN COMMUNE

(Acts 3, 4, 5)

CHAPTERS 3, 4, and 5 of the Acts of the Apostles are illustrations of the kind of community life which we were discussing in the last chapter.

If there is one thing the natural sciences agree on at the present time, it is that there is less and less of the fixed order which previous centuries thought to find in the universe, or in the processes of this planet. Skepticism about what the Bible calls "miracles" ("signs" in John's gospel) usually goes hand in hand with a rather naive view that nothing "out of the ordinary" ever happens in nature and, indeed, cannot do so. There is some truth to the assertion that the advance of knowledge, in the natural sciences and in medicine, merely underscores things *not* known and even adds to their number. By far the largest number of miracles recorded in the New Testament writings are healing miracles. It would be an indication of remarkable unsophistication on our part if we allowed ourselves to say, "That couldn't happen." Quite to the contrary, there are innumerable instances of sick people recovering from serious illnesses where there is no obvious explanation as to why this happened. Equally, there are countless people who fall ill, sometimes with serious disorders of mind and body, simply because they have "given up" or have even *willed* themselves into sickness.

At no point in the gospels does Jesus use the healings as anything more than "signs" of the impending reign of God. Certainly, he does not use them as "proof" of anything about *himself*. Time and time again, he emphasized that such healings are only one channel among others of God's power to make the dawning kingdom a reality to those who respond to it. There lies the element of faith—a total dependence on the power of God to act, if he so wills it.

There are people, men and women, who have possessed, and do now possess, an extraordinary capacity to evoke in others the response of faith to be open to God's healing power for mind and body. Continually, we are surrounded by miracle, in the natural order and in our lives. It is a sign of our own dulled apprehensions that we do not recognize "miracles" more often for what they truly are.

Only the most naive person, and, incidentally, the most unscientific then, is guilty nowadays of ruling out the possibility of "chance occurrences" in the natural order, or of dismissing out-of-hand the cure of the lame man which is recorded for us in Acts 3:1-10. For the author of Acts, and for Peter and John evidently, what was important was not a cure of an apparently hopeless case, but the agency through which that cure was accomplished. In any event, whether the address is genuine or whether Luke has used this occasion to insert into it an address by Peter on a fairly formal theme, the prime concern of the third chapter of Acts is the ability of Jesus to "save" men. All disorder in God's universe, whether it is physical or spiritual, is disruptive and in the end destructive of order and unity. The existence of human misery, human suffering, sickness and disease, along with sickness and disease in mind and spirit, are all offenses against the sovereignty of God. Peter declares that salvation, whether "natural" or "spiritual" is finally available to men through God's act in Jesus in the power of the Spirit.

In order to evaluate the resistance of the official Jewish community to the infant Church as illustrated for us in Acts 4, it is necessary to remind ourselves again that the Christian community was at this time still a small sect on the fringes of Judaism. To this extent, therefore, the Sanhedrin, the official governing body of Judaism, could—and did—treat the events recorded for us as being just another annoyance to be either tolerated or ignored. At any rate, the events were of no more final significance than incidents associated in times past with other "messianic movements." Peter and John, on being summoned to account for the disturbing outbreak of enthusiasm in the temple, were treated primarily as nuisances. They were warned that the kind of teaching they were doing was likely to lead to trouble for themselves and their followers. They were dismissed with a warning, the court evidently finding itself somewhat at a loss to know how to deal with this latest outburst of messianism. Incidentally, it is worth noting that one of the phrases (Acts 4:13) which has often been translated in the past as "ignorant men" is an extremely poor translation.[1] What astonished the Sanhedrin was the boldness with which men who were untrained in rabbinic law could face a court of such prestige and influence as the Sanhedrin.

The chapter concludes with a further reference to, and emphasis on, the element of unity and community of property so characteristic of the Jerusalem Church. It is this community of property which is used to introduce Barnabas, later on a close companion of Paul. How long this community of property persisted as a feature of the Jerusalem Church we have no means of knowing. We do hear later on in the Acts and in Paul's letters of a community of concern on the part of congregations elsewhere for the victims of the famine which afflicted the Jerusalem community during Paul's ministry.[2] It should be pointed out again that community of property is something which, obviously, is possible only in comparatively small organizations. It was certainly characteristic of one group of the Essenes. There seems to have been no attempt to reproduce this Jerusalem feature in other Christian congregations, although Paul's letters are insistent upon the obligation of Christians mutually to support each other in necessity.

The story of the man and woman in Acts 5 who gave lip service to the Jerusalem ideal of community of property, but who, at the same time, were bent upon deception, certainly reads very oddly to our ears. No very useful purpose is served by moralizing about the real or supposed fairness or equity of the judgment called down by Peter upon this unhappy couple. Equally certainly, no useful purpose is served by saying boldly that the ensuing deaths of Ananias and Sapphira "could not have happened." The slightest knowledge of the sometimes startling results of deep psychological shock should be enough to prevent us making easy judgments about what could, or could not, have happened in an instance such as this.

The fifth chapter of Acts closes with another story

of an appearance of the apostles before the Sanhedrin. Unquestionably, the teaching of the apostles was providing plenty of opportunity for curiosity seekers, as well as plenty of thought for those who came to listen out of genuine concern. The story of the imprisonment of the apostles indicates—as we have emphasized before—the manner in which the Jewish authorities tried to deal with what they saw as a pressure group of little more than nuisance value. (The movement had not spread very far, since the apostles and their followers found it possible to gather in one of the smaller areas of the temple which held two to three thousand people.) The account of the release of the apostles from prison provides some possible difficulties in that the word commonly translated "angels" in our English Bible can often mean simply "messenger." It is not always easy, even when the expression used is "the angel of the Lord," to discern whether the messenger is one of those heavenly beings whom we are accustomed to call "angels."[3]

The account of the deliverance of the apostles from prison, whether the agent of their release was human or not, must have goaded the Sanhedrin to exasperation and even fury. In acting as spokesmen for the apostles, Peter is represented as giving a very brief summary of what we have seen to be the apostolic *kerygma*. The scene is most noteworthy for the introduction of the figure of Gamaliel. He was the grandson of one of the most famous Jewish teachers of all time, Hillel the Elder. Moreover, it is apparent that Gamaliel was, at one time, Paul's teacher, and Paul's letters often bear all the marks of the interpretative method[4] which was introduced by Hillel the Elder into teaching the Law.[5] Gamaliel's advice to the Sanhedrin, valid for its own time and occasion, is still worth pondering for our purposes and questionings now.

The apostles, then, together with their followers were treated by the Sanhedrin as possessing an exasperating nuisance value and were—according to Jewish law—flogged and released with a warning not to continue teaching.

NOTES

1. The New English Bible renders this "untrained laymen," the Jerusalem Bible uses "uneducated laymen."

2. Acts 11:27-30, 24:17. Romans 15:26-28. I Corinthians 16:1-4. II Corinthians 8. Galatians 2:10.

3. It is imperative to note that in the Old Testament—at least in the older parts of it—God's "messengers" or "angels" are usually understood *at first* as being human beings. Genesis 18:1-14 is instructive in this regard. The "cherubim" of Exodus 25, for example, were certainly figures of the winged bulls so well known to us from Assyrian antiquity, and equally certainly *not* the winged infants depicted by Sir Joshua Reynolds in his paintings! It was only very gradually, mostly in response to Persian influence, that Hebrew thinking began to assimilate the idea of a wholly separate order of beings, attendant upon God as messengers. The simpering figures we know from the Victorian era would hardly have been recognized by Old Testament writers as "angels."

4. The interested reader will find a full discussion of this matter in Saul Lieberman, *Hellenism in Jewish Palestine*. New York: Jewish Theological Seminary of America, 1950. Or, in Hermann Strack, *Introduction to the Talmud and Mishnah*. Philadelphia: Jewish Publication Society of America, 1959.

5. It is sometimes said that the followers of Hillel the Elder were more "liberal" in their interpretation of the law of Moses than those who followed the teaching of Shammai, whose career overlapped that of Hillel the Elder. Although it is certainly true that the disciples of Hillel took a rather more liberal view with respect to the divorce proceedings of the Mosaic law over against the stricter requirements of the "school" of Shammai, it is not easy to make broad distinctions and it is certainly best to avoid the kind of suggestion sometimes made that the attitudes of the apostle Paul were shaped by a possible "liberalism" which owed its origin to Hillel the Elder through Paul's teacher Gamaliel.

5. ANOTHER GOOD SAMARITAN?
(Acts 6, 7:1-54)

WE COME now to the institution of a particular kind of ministry in the Jerusalem Church. The institution of the Seven as a ministry subordinate to the apostles, a ministry concerned with providing for the secular "welfare" of poorer members of the community, is sometimes seen as the foundation of what in later ages came to be called the "diaconate." There is, in fact, no evidence to support this contention and the word "deacon" does not appear in this story of the choosing of the seven. Certainly, the word "service" does appear in the Greek, and the word deacon means, strictly, "a servant." Perhaps, when the word deacon does appear later on in the New Testament books,[1] there was by that time a looking back to the institution of the Seven, although we do not know precisely what the links were. For example, in the city of Rome from quite early times the number of deacons attached to the bishop was limited to seven. Here, there must be a conscious looking back to the record as it is in the sixth chapter of Acts.

Of the men mentioned in the list of the Seven, three are of some importance. Philip was later on a zealous and apparently accomplished preacher of the gospel and a missionary of considerable courage. Stephen has always loomed large in the history of the Church as being its first martyr—its first "witness" by death to the belief in Jesus as Lord and Messiah. A third, Nicholas, may well be the later founder of a separated body which gave a good deal of trouble to one of the congregations in Asia Minor, a body to which John makes reference in the book of Revelation.[2] Of the others, we know nothing and they do not appear again in our New Testament records.

You will notice at the beginning of the story that there is a distinction made between "Hellenists" and "Hebrews." While both groups of people were integral parts of Judaism, what appears to be the distinction here is that Hellenists were Jews whose preferred language, and even possibly some points of custom, was Greek. About the term "Hebrews," there is, at this point, a considerable amount of doubt. I shall suggest to you, when we discuss Stephen, that the term "Hebrews" may very well mean Samaritans who had become Christians and not necessarily Jews who spoke Aramaic and were accustomed to using Hebrew in synagogue worship.

The enthusiasm with which Stephen went about his own particular contribution to the work of the Seven very soon brought him into severe conflict with Jews who could no longer tolerate what appeared to be a curiously ambivalent attitude of Stephen towards the Law of Moses. Very soon, Stephen found himself accused of deliberate propaganda both against the law and against the institution of the temple itself.

Most of Chapter 7 in Acts is taken up with what at first appears to be a speech by Stephen in his own defense. Some work in recent years by a very distinguished Jewish scholar (the late Dr. Abram Spiro, of Wayne State University) has raised some extremely important and interesting questions with regard to this chapter and with regard to the person of Stephen himself. It will be best for the reader to look at some of the important points of Spiro's interpretation of Acts 7 and then read the material in that chapter to see how much light the suggestions shed on this so-called "speech" of Stephen. The important points are:[3]

1. The whole so-called "speech" of Stephen in Acts 7 can only be understood when it is examined on the supposition that Stephen was a Samaritan who had been converted to faith in Jesus as Messiah.

2. Many of Stephen's quotations from Scripture depend upon purely Samaritan texts of the Old Testament.

3. Stephen's understanding of history from Abraham through Moses depends upon the Samaritan book of Exodus which contains a passage composed of selections from Deuteronomy and called by Samaritans the "tenth commandment."

4. Abraham is absolutely central to this piece of Samaritan-Christian propaganda which may well have issued from Stephen himself. This piece of propaganda is concerned above everything else to demonstrate the centrality of Abraham in all understanding of Hebrew history. In contrast, the place of Moses in the scheme of history outlined in Acts 7 is consistently downgraded. It was always a matter of great concern to the Samaritans that their own ancestry was "mixed" and they felt the necessity of appealing to Abraham as their "father."

5. The reference to "this place" in verse 7 (a composite of two half verses: Genesis 15:14a and Exodus 3:12b) is a deliberate change from the word "mountain." "This place" is standard Samaritan vocabulary for the place of the Samaritan shrine of Shechem, Mount Gerizim. This material even changes the words of the Prophet Amos (Amos 5:27) by making the prophet speak of an exile to Babylon, instead of the prophet's own use of the word Damascus. In other words, the sins of the Jews were visited upon them by the Babylonian Exile.

6. This passage also changes the text in Joshua 24:26 in order to speak of "tent" instead of a "sanctuary." Moreover, this Samaritan tract actually moves the place of the tent from Shechem to the nearby Mount Gerizim.

7. Stephen's material lays at the door of David the supreme heresy of seeking a "dwelling place" for God, instead of the "tent" which moved with the Israelites through the wilderness and was at this time—as always—the movable shrine of the Samaritans.

8. The material charges further that the temple of Solomon was not only in the wrong "place" but was of human construction (Acts 7:48-50).

9. Consistently, the phrase "our fathers" is used. It has been known for a long time that this phrase was standard Samaritan usage to describe an ancestry which they sought to appropriate to themselves and going back to Abraham.

10. Not only is Moses downgraded in this material in contrast to Abraham, but also it is noteworthy that Stephen devotes to the Mosaic law only one verse (Acts 7:38). In contrast with the long Old Testament account of the giving of the law, the law becomes of minor importance in Stephen's hands.

Stephen had no interest in the cultic worship of the Jerusalem temple—in fact, in common with the Essenes, he plainly regarded the Jerusalem temple as an illegitimate and futile exercise. It was being used by Judaism as a substitute for salvation. In general, the Samaritans had difficulty in accommodating the hope of a Messiah to the only books of our Old Testament which they accepted— that is to say, the first five books, generally called the Pentateuch. They had to be satisfied with the idea of a future prophet like Moses (Deuteronomy 18:15) and their own later preferred word for the Messiah—*taheb*—came to mean "one who returns" and took on all the characteristics of a composite figure combined of some features of Moses and some of Joshua.

We must now notice that Stephen is identified in Acts with a ministry to a group of people described in Greek as *Hellenistae*. You will remember that it was the widows belonging to this group who were suspected of receiving preferential treatment as over against their Hebrew speaking counterparts.[4] Sometimes the word *Hellenistae* has been translated or understood to mean "Greek speaking Jews" and sometimes rendered in English as "Grecians." This kind of translation or understanding is not really adequate. Any Jew living in Palestine in New Testament times, and, in fact, for some time before the ministry of Jesus, would be accustomed to using Greek in the ordinary conduct of day-to-day living. There were large numbers of Jews who, consciously or unconsciously, had taken over Greek methods of argument and logical analysis and a considerable number of Jews who had become "hellen-ized" to the extent of taking an interest in Greek literature and Greek drama. Some—especially in the period from 180 to 165 B.C.—had (to use a modern expression) sold out to the onward rush of Greek civilization. Certainly, many, in so doing, denied their Jewish heritage altogether and made a complete accommodation to Hellenistic cul-ture. And it must not be forgotten that there were large numbers of Jews living in the Mediterranean world whose *only* language was Greek, for whom the Hebrew scriptures had long ago been translated into Greek and whose whole way of thinking—apart from religious and ethnic identity—was entirely Greek. To us, accustomed to the idea of the Christian church as a supranational body, there may be something strange in the idea that such hellenized Jews should have found themselves a focus of active dislike, distrust, and even near persecution when they returned to the land of their fathers. But this seems to be the only way in which we may understand adequately the Greek word which Luke uses in Acts 6:1. There was bitter conflict between native Palestinian Jews, whose religious and cultural language was Aramaic and Hebrew, and completely hellenized Jews, who came back to Palestine either permanently or on pilgrimage with no religious or cultural language apart from Greek. It is not difficult, in light of what we have seen above about the Samaritans, to find some kind of alliance between Stephen and the Hellenists. Stephen would certainly have been sympa-thetic to any group which found itself ostracized or at best ignored and misunderstood by those whose adherence was to Jerusalem-centered orthodoxy, and whose lan-guage was Aramaic and Hebrew.

While it is easy to exaggerate and to get out of proportion this dispute between two groups within the early Christian community, there is no particular gain to be had in treating the early Christian community as though it was an ideal society, ignoring the very real differences and the many "party" squabbles that broke out from time to time and often assumed deeply bitter proportions.

NOTES

1. Philippians 1:1; I Timothy 3:8-13   2. Revelation 2:1-7; see also verses 12-17   3. For a more complete discussion, see *The Anchor Bible,* Vol. 31, *op. cit.,* Appendix V   4. Acts 6:1

6. THE FEAST OF STEPHEN

(Acts 7:55-60; 8)

THE TRIAL—if such it was—of Stephen by the Sanhedrin ended in his being stoned to death. This account of Stephen's death is notable for two things. First, we are here introduced to Paul—under his Jewish name of Saul—as a witness to this official act of execution for blasphemy. It is also notable for a rather puzzling sidelight on the crucifixion of Jesus. It has been asserted more than once, and within recent years by some notable non-Christian scholars, that at the time of the trial of Jesus the Sanhedrin had no authority to pass the death sentence, yet in Stephen's death we have an example of an execution strictly in accordance with the provisions of the Mosaic law. It seems entirely within the bounds of possibility that this stoning of Stephen was a result of action taken by the Sanhedrin during the absence from the scene of the Roman Procurator. It does not appear to be entirely satisfactory to regard the death of Stephen as simply a response to mob violence.

The death of Stephen, according to Luke, resulted in widespread agitation against the new sect (which had not yet achieved for itself the name "Christians"), and, as a result of agitation in Jerusalem, everyone fled from the city "except the Apostles." While we may say something later on about the position and status of the Apostles in later Church organization, this is a convenient point at which to remark that our own view of apostolic activity after the resurrection has been almost entirely colored by what we know of Paul. It seems very unlikely that the apostles ever engaged in any kind of extensive evangelistic activity. The first missionary activity outside Jerusalem of which we have any record is unequivocally declared to be the work of Philip, who was one of the Seven.

We learn at this point in the story that Philip—together with many others who had escaped from Jerusalem—went into Samaria. We are so accustomed to drawing broad conclusions from the incident recorded by John[1] about Samaritans and Jewish attitudes toward Samaritans, that we fail to take into account that there must have been some approval on the part of Jesus for preaching and teaching among Samaritans for Philip and his companions ever to have undertaken such a bold step at this point in the history of Christianity. Not only does Luke record the kind of manifestations by way of healings which he records in other places as accompanying the preaching of the gospel, he also records for us that the Samaritans received the message of the gospel, and the proclamation of the Messiah, with an enthusiastic welcome.

At this point we are also introduced to the mysterious character, Simon Magus—or Simon the Magician. Simon's title, given to him by the Samaritans, does not come across very well in our modern English translations.[2] Professor W. F. Albright preferred to use the phrase "the so-called great power of God." The phrase "so-called" does not

imply here, as it so very often does in our English, a sense
of condemnation, but rather an attempt to explain that
Simon claimed for himself the title "great power of God."

Simon's title as "the great power of God" (so far as
we can judge from later writings from orthodox Christian
sources) sprang from his own belief that he was a kind
of intermediary between God and men through his control
of divine messengers or angels. At times, he apparently
claimed to be God in human flesh; at other times, an
angel appearing in the guise of a human being. It is not
easy, in spite of the discoveries of speculative—even wildly
speculative—writings of a semi-Christian character which
have been made in recent years at Nag Hammadi (Cheno-
boskion) in Egypt, to determine just how far the second
and third century Christian writers were accurate in their
information about Simon the Magician. (The whole problem has not been made easier by the discovery at Nag
Hammadi of the "Gospel of Thomas," which *may* include
sayings of Jesus not otherwise known to us.[3]) That there
was a great deal of speculation on the fringes of both
Judaism and Hellenism about "astral determinism," and
that there was likewise a good deal of dabbling—some of
it very malicious—in what may loosely be called magic,
is well known to any student of New Testament times and
the first centuries of our own era. Speculation on the part
of both Jews and pagans about the precise relationship
of human events to beings who might be supposed to
belong to another sphere of existence, together with speculation about the precise manner in which stars and
planets might be thought to determine human hehavior
was all part of a very confused semiliterate or even, at
some levels, of literate philosophy.

What is certain is that something must have given
initial impetus to a whole system of speculation which
later came to be known to Church historians as "Gnosticism." It is not a simple matter to unravel the many con-

fusing and varied strands which went into the making up of this particular kind of speculation.[4] As its name implies, it was concerned with how man could come to "know" God. What seems to have been a constant feature in all the Gnostic systems was the belief that God was immeasurably remote from the affairs of men, and that he was so holy as to render the idea unthinkable that he should have any dealings directly with sinful humanity. Gnosticism, therefore, in most of its forms, spoke of a whole series of emanations from the Godhead to men, with each emanation from the fullness of the Godhead becoming a little less divine, a little less heavenly, than the emanation immediately preceding it. It is as though a stepladder was conceived as existing between God and men, with the very lowest rung in the ladder being allotted to beings who had some contact with sinful humanity. Any speculation which adds to it a possible historical circumstance always has a plausibility and an appeal which it would otherwise lack. Perhaps we may discern that Simon the Magician was a religious genius of some dimensions, however illiterate or literate he may have been. But if Simon the Magician was the "founding father" of the gnostic system of speculation which later fastened itself onto orthodox Christianity, then we may infer that Philip's preaching of God's act in Jesus—however tentatively Philip may have approached the theological concept of "incarnation"—will have provided Simon with an historical figure (namely Jesus) who could give to this embryonic speculation some kind of historical respectability. Without such New Testament statements as "God was in Christ reconciling the world to himself,"[5] it is very difficult to see how gnosticism could have blossomed later into the extremely flourishing enterprise which it eventually became. We may be justified, therefore, in accepting as basically true the contention of second and third century Christian writers that Simon the Magician can in some way be regarded as the one who gave form and substance to whole realm of gnostic thinking.

It has already been pointed out that Luke had a considerable interest in what may be described as the paranormal manifestations which attended the early evangelizing efforts of the Christian community. It is not surprising, therefore, to discover that Simon the Magician, who had undoubtedly attempted to exercise magical arts in the pursuit of his career of speculative ideas, was considerably attracted by the miraculous events which accompanied the preaching and baptizing mission of Philip. In any event, the arrival of Peter and John as a mission from the apostles in Jerusalem to give approval to what was being done by Philip only served to excite the wonder of Simon even more. Having accompanied Philip, and having seen, according to Luke's account, that the laying on of hands by the apostles carried with it as accompaniment extraordinary possession by the Holy Spirit, Simon sought by means of bribery to achieve this "power" for himself. We may be allowed to wonder how deep his own conversion had been and we may wonder at the motive which had brought Simon to baptism in the first place. But this kind of investigation is at best purely speculative, and Luke contents himself with the rebuff which Simon received at the hands of the Apostles. If later Church tradition is credible,[6] then Peter's restoration of Simon to repentance had no permanent or lasting effect.

This particular section of Acts ends with the account of Philip baptizing an Ethiopian eunuch who had been on pilgrimage to Jerusalem. The eunuch was long known in the middle East in court circles, even well into the Christian era. His status as one who lacked masculine powers (either by selfcastration or by having this disability imposed upon him) made the eunuch a man who often wielded considerable authority in court circles, his very disability rendering him safe from the customary intrigues among the womenfolk of any royal court. The eunuch was unable, of course, to produce a bastard child by a queen or a princess of a royal household and so posed no threat to any dynasty. We may, therefore, assume that the Ethiopian eunuch who was traveling in his carriage back to his own country was a man of considerable eminence at court.

Two things are of interest here. One is that this is again an indication of the concern which Luke always showed for Gentiles, both in his gospel and in Acts. Here is Philip acting as missionary to someone who was by ethnic consideration entirely outside the fold of Judaism. That he was attracted to Judaism seems to be clear from his having gone to Jerusalem on pilgrimage. But already— so Luke seems to be saying—there is being raised the question of the admission of Gentiles to this new Messianic community. The second interesting consideration arising from this passage is the introduction by Luke of a quotation from Isaiah 53.[7] The whole of Isaiah 53 has been, throughout the centuries, a source of meditation and inspiration to Christians as they have prayed over and thought about the redeeming ministry of Jesus. Whether Luke, at this point, is reporting an historical incident, or whether he is introducing the concept of the "suffering servant" as a theological explanation which was later given to Christians about the redeeming work of Jesus, we do not know. Some New Testament scholars have denied that the whole complex of "Servant Songs" in Isaiah was ever used by Jesus in explanation of his own ministry and person. This seems to the present writer to be altogether too skeptical a judgment, and, whether this account of Philip and the Ethiopian eunuch is historically accurate or not, the writer feels no hesitation in saying that the theological understanding of Jesus' mission as "servant" belongs to the earliest strata of Christian tradition and, ultimately, to Jesus himself.

It will be noticed that the Ethiopian courtier, after hearing Philip explain the ministry and mission of Jesus, asks to be received into the messianic community by baptism. Attention has already been called to the importance of baptism and to its possible origin in Essene practice, but it is interesting to note that some ancient manuscripts of the Acts of the Apostles incorporate a caution by Philip which may well have come from early baptismal liturgies. Philip's question to the new convert is preserved at what is verse 37 in the King James version of the New Testament—Philip asks, or seeks to make sure, that the convert believes with all his heart. The Ethiopian courtier is represented in some late versions of the text as replying, "I believe that Jesus-Messiah is the Son of God."[8] Undoubtedly, early converts to the Christian community must have been required to make some statement of belief in the messianic mission and ministry of Jesus, especially when those converts came to the Christian community from Judaism. Later on, when we find Paul producing phrases like "Jesus is Lord," we are on the very threshold of the kind of theological statement which was later to be enshrined in what we now call "creeds."

It is difficult to say by what method Luke incorporated some of the episodes in the early chapters of Acts, or what means he pursued in order to gather together traditions about the early days of the Christian community as it was centered in Jerusalem and spread outwards to Samaria and the surrounding countryside. There is a selectivity about episodes such as this one which suggests that Luke found a whole mass of reported incidents and traditions which were streamlined to produce a kind of "typical" picture of the Church in its beginning days in Jerusalem. After this episode, Luke's narrative moves into something far more connected and smooth flowing. It is at this juncture that Luke takes up the dramatic change in fortune, and the equally dramatic change in direction of the Church, occasioned by the conversion of Saul the Pharisee.

NOTES

1. John 4.
2. Acts 8:10. New English Bible: "The Great Power." Jerusalem Bible: "the divine power that is called Great."
3. For a discussion of Gnosticism and the Gospel of Thomas, see Robert M. Grant, *The Secret Sayings of Jesus*. Dolphin Books, 1960.
4. For a fuller treatment, see J. W. C. Wand, *The Four Great Heresies*. London: A. R. Mowbray & Co., 1955.
5. II Corinthians 5:19.
6. Opposing views on this tradition may be seen in F. L. Cross, ed. *Oxford Dictionary of the Christian Church*. Oxford University Press, 1958, p. 1258.
   John D. Davis, ed., *Westminster Dictionary of the Bible*. Philadelphia: Westminster Press, 1944, p. 568.
7. Acts 8:32-33.
8. This verse is mentioned only in the footnotes of the New English and Jerusalem Bibles.

7. INTERSTATE 22 TO DAMASCUS

(Acts 9:1-19)

THE CONVERSION of Saul the Pharisee to Christianity brought to the infant Church a totally new dimension—cosmopolitan society, as distinct from the somewhat narrow provincialism of Jerusalem-based Judaism. We should not, however, exaggerate this kind of contrast because Jerusalem was never, in any sense of the term, cut off from the main stream of life and thought in the rest of the Mediterranean world. It was always very self-conscious of its own dignity as the center of Judaism and to a greater or lesser degree had always resisted the incursion of too much foreign influence.

Paul tells us that he was a Roman citizen, free born,[1] of the city of Tarsus, the capital of Cilicia. Cilicia was a large, rich, agricultural region, the city of Tarsus being a center of manufacture for linen cloth and tents made of goat hair. (The material for making the tents was actually named after the province.) Tarsus, a major port for the transshipping of all kinds of goods from eastern Anatolia, became the capital of the province of Cilicia around 65 B.C. Not only was Tarsus a "free city"—that is to say, it was free of imperial taxation—it was also a great educational center. Many professional educators went on from Tarsus to Rome to practice their professions there.

Paul, in saying he was a free born citizen, probably meant that his father had been granted Roman citizenship. His father may have been a descendant of a group of Jews who were very influential in the business world in that part of the Mediterranean under the successors of Alexander the Great. It is likely that Paul's Roman name (Paulus) was the name of the Roman citizen who had granted citizenship to Paul's father. There has been a considerable amount of discussion in times past about Paul's full name. About his Jewish name, there is no question—it was Saul, which made the apostle a member of the tribe of Benjamin. One very prominent historian in the last century suggested that the apostle's Roman name was, in full, Gaius Julius Paulus. Generally speaking, the first name of a Roman citizen corresponded to what we would call a "Christian" name, the middle name told the Roman clan or tribe to which the citizen belonged, and the last name marked off the person as an individual. Paul (Paulus) was a fairly common first name, but we don't know what the apostle's family name was. What is very puzzling is why Luke uses the name Saul in Acts right up to the time of the apostles' meeting with the Roman governor of Cyprus (Acts 13:7). To this puzzle we have no complete answer, and—since there seems to be no particular reason for Luke's practice—we can only suppose that Luke is being faithful to the sources of information which he received.

Occasionally, it has been said that Paul's letters, and the cosmopolitan air which runs through them, is proof that Paul was once a student at the university of Tarsus. There is no proof whatsoever for this statement. There is, for example, no indication in Paul's letters that he had ever received an education which was at all similar to a formal Greek education in philosophy, mathematics, and rhetoric. What *is* true is that Paul was well enough prepared to use the common figures of speech, ordinary illustrations from law and day to day practice, wherever the occasion suited him. The fact that Paul could use lists of virtues and vices, such as might be found in the writings of Stoic philosophers, does no more than indicate that Paul, with the ordinary education of his time, had an ear attuned to the necessities of the occasion for which he was writing or speaking. Paul's own statement about his education is that he was brought up in Jerusalem by the famous rabbi Gamaliel.[2] We have already met Gamaliel, the grandson of Hillel the Elder, and since Hillel the Elder was responsible for introducing into rabbinic discussion the Greek rules and customs of interpretation, we may assume that Paul's education in rabbinic commentary on the Law was painstaking and thorough. We can see two methods of interpretation of scripture at work in Paul's letters, one of them is a rather free ranging "sermon" type of exhortation around the events of the Old Testament and the ministry of Jesus and the other is a most painstaking and exhaustive attention to the meaning of precise words and phrases which we may assume Paul to have inherited from Gamaliel.

The account of Paul's conversion, with its dramatic word pictures, we can read for ourselves. Luke plainly felt that this event was of enormous significance for the early Christian Church, since the account is given not only here but also on two other occasions in Acts.[3] It is necessary for us to deal here with two questions closely linked with this story of the conversion. First, why did Paul, immediately after the execution of Stephen, request letters of permission from the Jerusalem clergy to seek out members of this small body of messianic enthusiasts? Up to this moment, we do not hear of any movement of missionaries into the region around Damascus. It is possible to assume, as some scholars have, that the Essenes with their deep seated longing for the messianic age, had provided the early Christian community with an influential number of converts.[4] In addition, we know certainly that Damascus was a center for Essenes at this time and had been for sometime past. Possibly, Paul was of the opinion that Essene enthusiasm, if it provided this new sect with converts, ought to be curtailed.

Secondly, we may ask how we are to interpret the word picture of the story of Paul's conversion as it is given in Acts 9. While undoubtedly there have been instances in Christian history of sudden and dramatic conversions from one way of life to another without apparent antecedents, we may question that this was the case with Paul. He was a witness at the execution of Stephen.[5] He knew how Stephen argued his case for Jesus being the expected Messiah (whether that case was argued by a "tract" or a "speech") and Paul may well have been more aware of the ministry and mission of Jesus than would appear from this account of his conversion. In any event, Paul, as a good Pharisee, was far more sympathetic to the idea of an expected Messiah, and far more sympa-

thetic to the notion of resurrection, than any Sadducee
could ever have been. It is possible, therefore, to understand this dramatic account of Paul's conversion as that
of a man traveling to Damascus and already beginning
to wrestle in mind and conscience with the awe-inspiring
possibility that, after all, Stephen was right and that
Jesus was indeed the expected Deliverer of Israel.

Perhaps not many of us have ever been privileged to
receive what is commonly called a vision. If we have, then
we shall have to express how this came to us in our own
words and in some way which will convey its essential
meaning to those who have some right to know. It may
be that visions are, in spite of our present industrial and
technological age, not so uncommon as many people
believe. Certainly there are many in our time for whom
the intellectual adventure has no appeal and for whom
the only access to any vision of reality is through the
highly dubious employment of mind expanding drugs. In
that way lies no vision in any true sense, but only a pained
awareness, whether good or evil, that man is not the
master of his own destiny. For Paul, the vision was an
illumination that he had been utterly and totally wrong.
On how many levels he had been wrong he tells us later,
in a letter he wrote to the Christians in the city of Rome,
when he wrote of the vocation of Israel. For the time
being it is enough to leave Paul as he approaches Damascus with the terrifying realization that his part in the
killing of Stephen had been completely wrong and that
the Jesus for whom Stephen had died was, indeed, the
Messianic Deliverer of Israel.

The word picture of Paul's conversion represents him
as being helpless and blind as he made his way, with
his companions, into the city of Damascus. There is no
escaping the plain words of Luke's statement that Paul
was temporarily blinded. However we seek to explain
Paul's physical blindness as a psychosomatic phenomenon,

it is easy to imagine the mental and spiritual distress which must have afflicted him as a result of this realization that so far he had been mentally and spiritually blind to the implications of the ministry of Jesus.

Many years later, the great bishop, theologian, and preacher, Augustine of Hippo, made use of the story of Paul's vision to drive home the lesson of the unity between Jesus and his Church. In commenting on the story of the conversion of Paul and the declaration of Jesus in Paul's vision ("I am Jesus, and you are persecuting me") Augustine says "the body is persecuted, and the head cries out in pain." It is too much to say that it was the experience of his conversion which made Paul refer so often in his letters to the Church as "the body of Christ," but it would certainly be safe to say that what came to Paul in this moment of illumination cannot have been without significance for the way in which later he spoke of the unity between Christ and the believer.

The account of Paul's reception in Damascus by Ananias is a completely straightforward account, notable for its introduction of the phrase "the way" as a description of the Christian community. While the phrase is peculiar to Luke in Acts, it is certainly an appropriate description of the Christian commitment as a way, a pilgrimage, to God undertaken in union with Jesus as Lord and Messiah. It was also employed by Jewish scholars, following the Old Testament, to describe man's journey to God.

NOTES

1. Acts 22:28.
2. Acts 22:3.
3. Acts 22:6-16.
   Acts 26:12-18.
4. Recent research on the very technical questions about the calendar of the passion and crucifixion of Jesus have convinced some scholars that Jesus and his disciples used the ancient solar

calendar of the *Book of Jubilees* and that this usage is reflected in the gospel accounts of the passion. All of this may well lead us to ask to what extent the early Christian community was dominated—in some cases at least—by interests carried over from sectarian practice. *Cf.* Matthew Black, "The Dead Sea Scrolls and Christian Origins," in *The Scrolls and Christianity*, ed. Matthew Black. New York: Charles Scribner's Sons.

5. Acts 7.

8. EDUCATION OF A CONVERT

(Acts 9:20-31)

THE ACCOUNT of Paul's conversion provides us with two notes: first, the astonishment felt in Damascus by those who knew beforehand of Paul's mission, who now heard him preaching Jesus as Messiah; secondly, the great difficulty encountered by anyone who tries to make a neat scheme of the chronology of the life and ministry of Paul. Looking at the end of the story of Paul's conversion[1] we could get the impression that Paul's attempt to go to Jerusalem to introduce himself to the rest of the Christian community, especially the apostles, was made almost immediately after his conversion. That this is not so, we discover from reading the account which Paul gives of his own movements in the letter that he wrote to Galatia.[2] Luke's only indication of Paul's journey into "Arabia" is in Acts 9:23. In order to save confusion later on, we must remember that Paul, after this initial preaching and teaching in Damascus, left the city to spend three years in "Arabia." This name indicates roughly what used to be called Trans-Jordan (nowadays the area includes the kingdom of Jordan), the country of the Nabataean Arabs.

Paul felt the need to be alone, to work out the implications for the future of a life which had now been radically and drastically changed by his acknowledgment of Jesus as Messiah. There was need for what military people call "drastic reappraisal." It is far too easy to assume—as some otherwise responsible people have done in years past—that during this period of three years Paul was not only completely alone, but also that by some mysterious means he achieved all his knowledge of the tradition of the life and ministry of Jesus, together with the theological implications which that life and ministry carried. This is much too naive and it is not a very intelligent way of regarding the means which God employs to increase our knowledge and devotion. It is certainly true that Paul brought to all his teaching and writing about the Christian faith profound insights into its implications both for his own time and for the future.

Nevertheless, it is necessary to insist that Paul's application of his new confession of Jesus as Messiah to a scriptural discipline which he had learned already as a student of Gamaliel would have provided him with a great deal of material for reflection. For example, we may take notice of Paul's exacting commentary on the figure of Adam as he understood it in the light of the ministry of Jesus.[3] But unless we are to suppose that Paul had spent his time in Jerusalem with a carefully constructed spy network seeking out every possible scrap of information on Christian belief and practice, it is necessary to ask how Paul discovered, for example, the tradition—which he "received"—about the Eucharist.[4] It is not very intelligent and not very helpful to respond to this kind of question by saying that, during those three years in Trans-Jordan, Paul learned the Christian tradition and learned of Christian practice through "visions." Paul himself was by no means the last Christian to insist that whatever validity there may be in "visions," it is necessary to be extremely cautious in using them to establish normative patterns of belief and behavior for Christians.

When, then, did Paul learn those elementary and fundamental patterns of Christian faith which he was later to apply with such distinction and expertise in his writings to Christian congregations? Where, we may ask, was he able to learn so much about the Christian practice of baptism that he was able to write and speak in such an illuminating way, a way which made great use of Old Testament figures of speech, later on in his teaching ministry?

It is possible that Paul's interest and concern in this matter of baptism may give us some indication as to where he spent some of this three year period of retreat. At this point, I think it is necessary for me to make some kind of apology or defense since I am about to suggest that Paul spent some of his time in residence with the Essene community at Qumran. The apology—or defense— is necessary because it is all too easy, in the light of the dramatic discovery of the Dead Sea Scrolls, to "see Essenes under every bush." Some New Testament scholars have enthusiastically embraced the identification of the Dead Sea Scrolls with the Essenes as a means of solving practically all of the outstanding questions in New Testament scholarship. Other New Testament scholars have wished to minimize almost to a vanishing point the influence of Jewish sectarianism on the New Testament. Insofar as it is possible to say so without prejudice, I have tried to steer something of a middle position between these two extremes, but any judgment as to how far I have been successful must be left to others.

Let us now return to this question of baptism. Both the word and the ideas associated with it figure quite largely in the New Testament writings, and, so far as we know, baptism—in the sense of ritual washing, whether self-administered or administered by others—was a feature of religious practice confined during New Testament times to the Essenes.[5] The New Testament is emphatic that a Christian is baptized "once for all," presumably in response to the fact that the redeeming work of Jesus was "once for all." The implications of a "once for all" baptism are not immediately apparent to us, since we stand at a point in time where we are accustomed to think of baptism as a single, never-to-be-repeated, occasion. The connection between baptism and the passion, death, and resurrection of Jesus was one which must have appeared as dramatic and all-embracing in its implications for any one who had known, or had heard of, the baptism administered by John the Baptizer. It is, therefore, possible that a knowledge of the antecedents of John the Baptizer, of the source from which he derived his practice of baptism, together with the knowledge that Christians continued the practice (though on a quite different basis of interpretation) may have driven Paul to see what there was to discover of Essene thought and practice at Qumran. In any event, something is necessary to explain the supreme confidence with which Paul set himself the task of explaining his new found faith to converts and also being able to defend himself before the apostles in Jerusalem when eventually he met with them.

We may doubt seriously whether God permits us to seize hold of new knowledge *merely* by flashes of insight. Initial flashes of insight are always important both to the scholar and to ordinary people, and the scientist is accustomed to making an hypothesis and then patiently pursuing ways and means to discover how far his original hypothesis can be proved. Nevertheless, it is important to remember that an initial flash of insight, or a scientific hypothesis, always arises from past experience even if we are forgetful of the past experience which produced the insight or the hypothesis.

Paul had returned to Damascus after his stay of three

years in Arabia, and, although everything appeared to be
working out well, there was evidence of a desire on the
part of some Jews in Damascus to get Paul out of the
way as quickly as possible, by death or any other means.
The indignity of Paul's escape from Damascus—being
lowered in a basket from the walls of the city at night—
must have been felt by Paul to have been somewhat less
than courageous since he refers to it in one of his letters.[6]
That Paul's attempt to commend himself to the Christian
community in Jerusalem was at first met with fear and
refusal, is very easy to understand. It must have been
felt that there was considerable doubt attaching to the
conversion of one who had lately been a most violent
opponent. Some of the fears—if not all of the reluctance—
seemed to have been allayed by Barnabas, who undertook
to sponsor Paul's cause to the apostles in Jerusalem. Here
once again, we are faced with an apparently irreconcilable
difference in the tradition between the incident as it is
recorded by Luke and the account given by Paul himself
in his letter to Galatia.[7] Either record may be at fault,
but it is more likely that Luke has been mistaken than
that Paul—with his vivid recollection of those early days—
had mistaken exactly what had happened. Paul was accepted to the extent that he was able to go around with
some of the apostles in Jerusalem, speaking and teaching
about his new found faith.

How long this lasted, we have no means of knowing,
but we are told that Paul, when he undertook to speak
to the "Hellenists," was greeted with violent opposition.
For the Hellenists, there were very different considerations at work from those which operated among Jews in
Damascus. As Jews brought up in a completely Greek
environment, whose language both in civil life and
probably in worship was almost certainly Greek, there
was the supreme necessity of proving their "Jewishness"
in the face of this phenomenon of a Hebrew-speaking

Pharisee who had suddenly thrown the whole picture of Judaism in Jerusalem into confusion. We must suppose that so intense was the desire of these Hellenists to prove their essential Jewishness (especially in Jerusalem) that they were determined to kill Paul and he was quietly taken out of the way. Paul was first taken to Caesarea and then sent off to his native Tarsus.

Paul's departure from Jerusalem for his home town of Tarsus brings us to a gap of some ten years in the story of Paul and these years of his life were spent in a ministry not only in Tarsus, but in the rest of Cilicia and in Syria. To this ten year ministry of evangelism Paul refers only three times.[8] If we read the account as it stands in Acts, we get very little indication of this extended ministry of evangelism. By the time Paul began what has come to be called his "first missionary journey" he was already an accomplished teacher and preacher.

NOTES

1. Verse 25.
2. Galatians 1:11 ffg.
3. Romans 5:12-14.
   I Corinthians 15:21-22.
4. I Corinthians 11:23-26.
5. C. S. Mann, *The Man for All Time*, p. 44. So far as our present knowledge goes, baptism was an Essene custom and the (self-administered) baptism of converts to Judaism did not arise until the end of the first century A.D. *Cf.* William F. Albright and C. S. Mann, "Qumran and the Essenes," in *The Scrolls and Christianity*. London: SPCK, 1969, pp. 11 ff.
6. II Corinthians 11:32-33.
7. Galatians 1:18-19.
8. Acts 9:30; 11:25.
   Galatians 1:21.

9. JAILBREAK
(Acts 9:32-43; 10; 11:1-18; 12:1-23)

LUKE NOW returns to the apostle Peter and again takes up the story of Peter's ministry to Jews and others who lived on the fringes of Judaism. As we have already seen, it is very difficult to reconstruct any kind of time sequence or chronology in this part of the Acts, and we have no way of knowing precisely how the following incidents fit into the ten year period in Paul's life to which we have already referred.

Once more, we are faced with "miracles of healing." And, once more, it is necessary to remind ourselves that we are not entitled, in what has come to be called "the age of science and technology," to adopt a superior and quasi-sophisticated attitude toward these accounts of extraordinary healings. Indeed, the further medicine and medical science progress, the less we appear to know of the relationships between mind and body. In modern medical discussions, we have become accustomed to speaking of psychosomatic conditions, but we tend to forget that there are undoubtedly conditions of sickness in some of the New Testament stories which should be described in the same terms. We do not know, for example, what had made Aeneas bedridden. Nor are we likely to discover at this distance in time why it was that the invocation of the name Jesus was sufficient to cure Aeneas. In a very real sense, asking such questions is as fruitless as asking why some people are cured by psychiatric care in our modern society when there would appear to be very little reason for a mental state to produce physical symptoms.

In the same way, we are not likely at this stage to be able to find out whether the woman Tabitha was really dead—or in a state of coma. We do know that excavated burials of those who died centuries ago have very often turned up indications of people who were buried in a coma and who must have recovered for a short time after burial. There is no need to go into this at any greater length, and this example is given here only to illustrate the uncertainty which people long ago must have felt as to whether someone was really in a state of coma or death. This is in no way to minimize the importance of what Luke records as resulting from the arrival and prayer of Peter. Any kind of skepticism which we care to bring to reading accounts of miraculous cures in the New Testament would seem to indicate that we should bring the same kind of skepticism to bear on the "miraculous" claims made by advertisers for their products on television and in the other media.

Chapter ten of Acts records for us an incident which at first sight would appear to set the stage for Paul's future ministry among Gentiles. This is not necessarily the case, however. Peter's visit to Cornelius the centurion is not a straightforward case of Peter preaching to pagans who had had no contact with belief in God as Jews understood such belief. The story makes it clear that Cornelius—like so many other persons born outside Judaism—was a "God-fearer" and, therefore, one who was well acquainted with the distinctive beliefs and way of life of Judaism. Exactly how much Cornelius knew of any kind of "messianic expectation" we do not know. Such messianic expectation, such prayer for active and decisive intervention by God for the salvation of men, was a matter which was interpreted in vastly different fashions by many sections of Judaism. Nevertheless, Luke spends a considerable amount of space on the visit of Peter to Cornelius, rightly concluding that this was, in many ways, an important step on the road to evangelizing those who stood on the fringes of Judaism.

What is interesting about the story as it is told is the account of Peter's vision. Evidently, Peter had already begun to give some consideration to the question of how those on the fringes of the synagogue should be treated if ever they came to make inquiries about the gospel. This was obviously no light question, and it is a useful indication of the way in which "Godfearers" were tolerated, indeed welcomed, by Jews but were, nevertheless, regarded as being strictly outsiders until and unless they took the step of becoming converted to Judaism by formal act, in the case of males by circumcision. But, in spite of Peter's vision of God's lordship over all men, and in spite of his conviction on this present occasion that the good news of God's act in Jesus applied to all men, he was left with many reservations on a later occasion.[1]

The later battle for the inclusion of Gentiles in the infant community of the gospel was only entering the stages of a preliminary skirmish. There was much serious fighting to be done on this front and it is probably not too much to say that it was not until the end of the first Jewish war, and the destruction of the temple in A.D. 70, that the battle for the inclusion of Gentiles in the Church on equal terms with Jews was won. Even so, what happened after A.D. 70 was not so much a victory for principle—the principle of the equal applicability of the message of salvation to Jew and Gentile—as it was the almost near-disappearance of Jewish Christianity from the scene.

Peter's speech (or homily as we might prefer to call it) to the household of Cornelius makes the solid theological point that God is the God of all men and that God's message of salvation must, in the last analysis, be of equal importance and equal application to all men. Nevertheless, Peter is able to assume on the part of his hearers an acquaintance with the Judaism in which he himself had been raised and, it is interesting to note, the content of this homily differs very little from the kind of thing which he is reported to have said in the earlier chapters of Acts. Attention has already been called to the doubts which have been raised from time to time about the historical accuracy of these speeches in Acts, but it is extremely difficult to imagine in what other terms such an address to Jews or Godfearers could possibly have been made.

Two other matters call for attention here. First, Luke records that the acceptance by Cornelius and his household of the message preached by Peter was accompanied by signs of joy and enthusiasm and a manifestation of extraordinary "signs" of the presence of the Holy Spirit. Attention has already been called to extraordinary signs of enthusiasm and excitement connected with the first Christian Pentecost. Luke keeps us constantly aware throughout Acts of these scenes of exhilaration and joy on the part of new Christian communities and—granted that in many cases these communities were Jews and people living on the fringes of Judaism—this kind of exuberant joy is exactly what we would expect when the hearers were confronted with news of a messianic ministry for which living witnesses were available. It may be doubted, however, how far the Christian Church could long survive on a diet of exuberance and enthusiastic manifestation. It is noteworthy that many years after the events recorded in Acts an attempt to revive such manifestations as a deliberate matter of Church policy very soon found the author of the movement separated from the Church and his followers in various stages of disarray about what were or were not the foundation facts of Christian belief.[2]

Secondly, Peter is reported by Luke to have found it necessary to defend himself before the Christian community in Jerusalem for his actions with regard to Cornelius and his family. This ought not to be a surprise to us. We must remind ourselves constantly that the movement of the Christian Church beyond the frontiers of Judaism was a very gradual process and Jewish Christians in Jerusalem were likely to be far more conservative in this respect than perhaps would be the case with Jews of the Dispersion, Jews who had long been accustomed to living in wholly Gentile surroundings. In any event, we would be mistaken if we regarded the baptism of Cornelius and his household as marking any radical new departure or an abrupt change of policy on the part of the infant Christian community.

In spite of the fact that other events are recorded by Luke as following upon the baptism of Cornelius, we will end this chapter with the account of Peter's deliverance from prison recorded by Luke in Acts 12. Up to this time, the apostles had been left more or less alone in Jerusalem and had not been compelled to flee the city in the disturbances that followed the killing of Stephen. But, in the final years of his reign, Herod was more and more anxious to court favor and began a selective persecution of some members of the Jerusalem community. We are told that he ordered the execution of James, John's brother—although on what pretext we do not know—and then had Peter arrested.

What are we to make of this deliverance of Peter from prison? It would certainly be possible to read the word "angel" in most of our English versions by the word "messenger" and make of Peter's escape from prison an affair which was contrived by someone who quite literally "sprang" Peter from jail. It is certainly possible to read the account as though this is what happened with very little by way of alteration of the text. Peter himself is represented as saying that "the Lord really did send his messenger and has saved me from Herod." But Luke's statement that this was a "messenger of the Lord" also may be meant to indicate that this was a miraculous deliverance accomplished by no mere human agency. Almost everything depends upon one's definition of "the miraculous." I do not wish to labor the point here but it is worth a reminder that we have all of us, at one time or another in our lives, been the objects of what in hind sight we might wish to refer to as a miraculous intervention of one kind or another.[3] Certainly, whether Peter's escape from prison was accomplished by human agency or by an angel, we must regard his being preserved for some years to come as being miraculous for the future continuity of the infant Christian community.

NOTES

1. Galatians 2:11-13   2. Montanus—2nd century A.D. "enthusiast"
3. Chapter IV

10.   A SECULAR CITY

(Acts 11:19-30; 12:24-25; 13:1-3)

WE NOW pick up again the threads of the ministry of the apostle Paul. Barnabas—to whom Paul must have been very heavily indebted for instruction in the oral tradition of the ministry of Jesus—went to Tarsus to look for Paul and brought him back to Antioch. In one way or another, Antioch was destined to be an extremely important center for Christian missionary endeavor throughout the ministry of Paul. It was here that Christians had come following the persecution occasioned by Stephen's death and had actually taken the step of preaching the faith to people whom Luke describes as "Greeks." In Luke's vocabulary, this can only mean pagan Greeks, not Hellenized Jews. We don't know on what kind of scale this preaching and teaching was done, but it is evident that Barnabas (who

was sent to Antioch on an evaluation mission by the
Jerusalem community) found nothing to criticize about
this rather bold step of teaching pagan Greeks.

Unfortunately for us, there were twenty-four cities in
the Roman Empire all bearing the name Antioch. The
city of Antioch with which we are now concerned had
a population in Paul's time of half a million or more and
was an extremely important communication center between Rome on the one hand and the Parthian empire
on the other. It boasted a mint, from which much of its
wealth was derived, and shared with two other cities the
honor of being placed second to the city of Rome in imperial importance. Moreover, Antioch was the center of
trade in luxury goods and in this respect was unlike any
other Roman city. Other Roman cities might derive their
wealth through ordinary business contacts, or through
the imperial staging service, or through the comings and
goings of merchant ships bearing the necessities of life,
but Antioch was responsible for shipping goods to Italy
from China, India, Babylonia, Persia, and Arabia. It was
no accident that, whenever the Roman emperor visited
the eastern part of his empire, it was Antioch that was
chosen for his headquarters. In magnificence and splendor
it is said to have been much more impressive than the
city of Rome. Its public buildings were on a far more
lavish scale, its main street—over four miles in length—
was paved with marble and was lined on either side with
marble colonnades. It had the unique distinction of being
the only city in the world at that time, so far as we know,
which lighted its streets at night.

Antioch, however, was situated at a rather uneasy
crossroads between the Roman empire and the Parthians
to the East. A good deal of Roman policy at that time,
and for many years following, was dictated by making
provision for any possible advance of the Parthians westward. The province of Syria (of which Antioch was the

capital) was of tremendous importance in the Roman scheme of things and the military authority of the governor of Syria extended not only over that province but also a good deal of Asia Minor. If ever the Parthians were suspected of making moves to the West, the whole imperial defense of that part of the Mediterranean would fall on the governor of Syria.

As we might expect, Antioch was the regular meeting place of the leading citizens and important civic officials for all the cities of the province of Syria. We can, therefore, imagine the tremendous amount of coming and going and the bustle of activity which constantly characterized Antioch in the days of Paul and the early Christian missions. Paul and Barnabas deliberately used Antioch as a base from which to conduct the extensive missionary enterprises with which Paul's name is linked. Throughout the ministry of Paul, the Parthians were not disposed to face a showdown with the Roman Empire and the early Christian missions were conducted from Antioch against a background of security and the prospect of an extended peace.

Paul's consistent missionary strategy was to go from one capital city of a province to the lesser "regional" cities and in each place, if possible, to establish a solid Christian community from which the message of the gospel could be carried to other communities. In the case of Antioch, the advantages of using the city as a base are obvious. On the other hand, it is well to remember that there were some solid disadvantages about Antioch, as well as advantages which belonged to the status of the city itself. Visited as it was by every conceivable kind of official, trader, tourist, and the ordinary curiosity seeker, Antioch attracted to itself the same kind of reputation as Corinth. There were religious shrines in profusion in Antioch, notably the shrine of Daphne, a shrine much visited and known to be the center of an oracle, a shrine where visitors on payment of a fee could receive guidance (usually couched in extremely vague terms) on a variety of topics.

There existed in Antioch, side by side, innumerable manifestations of religious practice, the imperial authority with its vast bureaucracy, and a whole cosmopolitan population drawn from all corners of the empire. It is well here to add one small word of warning. We often hear (thanks to the well known book of that title) of the "secular city."[1] Sometimes we assume, incorrectly, that the cities of medieval Christendom were in some sense or other "religious" cities, in strong contrast with the cities which we know today and in strong contrast to the cities of later Romano-Greek civilization. In fact, for all the multiplicity of shrines, temples, churches, and other such objects of popular devotion, the city in the history of civilization has always been a purely secular affair. Perhaps there has in all of history been only one city to which the title "secular" could not be given without some qualification—the city of Jerusalem. Notoriously, the experience of most cities is that, in spite of the buildings given over to worship of one kind or another, attendance at shrines and religious devotions is at best meager and half-hearted. Antioch was no better, and certainly no worse, than any other affluent city within the confines of the Roman Empire. Nevertheless, it was to such Roman cities that Paul deliberately turned his steps with conscious determination to found in them, if it was at all possible, a solidly based Christian community.

Antioch, thus, became the center of Christian missionary enterprise. It was from Antioch that Paul carried the message of the gospel westward throughout the Roman world and eventually to Rome itself. After Jerusalem fell in A.D. 70, Antioch became the center of missionary enterprise directed towards the East and it was from

Antioch that the gospel spread through the Parthian Empire into India and China.

One of the thoughts which constantly goes through the mind of the author as he thinks back on the missionary work of Paul and the early Christians is the way in which the spread of the gospel illustrates the difference between two Greek words, both of which have a distressing tendency to be translated by the word "power" in English. One of those words is *dunamis*, which, so often in Greek, can mean the naked exercise of secular calculation. The other word is *exousia*, which is separated from *dunamis* by being referred more often to the endeavors of mind and spirit. Antioch, like so many cities before and since, amply illustrated the word *dunamis*.

Barnabas and Paul carried on a year's work of evangelization in Antioch and Luke tells us that it was in this city that members of this new community were first called "Christians." We are so accustomed to the word as a description for those of us who have given ourselves in allegiance to the community which Jesus founded, that community which embodies God's act of redemption in Jesus, that we seldom, if ever, stop to ask ourselves what other word might be used to describe us. We are not told by Luke whether the term was a compliment or an insult, but if we translate it as "Messianists," we may easily conjecture that it was applied as a somewhat scornful description of this new sect which believed that God's Messiah was identified with Jesus of Nazareth.

It was during the time of the ministry of Barnabas and Paul in Antioch that a great famine occurred in the Roman Empire, with particular force in the eastern Mediterranean, and the Christian community in Antioch sent contributions of money to the Jerusalem Church. (There are some difficulties here about the chronology of Paul's life. This discussion has been deferred to an appendix at the end of this book). After this brief journey to Jerusalem the two missionaries took up their work again in Antioch until, as we are told, the Holy Spirit chose Barnabas and Paul for work elsewhere. We don't know how this kind of decision was reached. Perhaps it was suggested by Christians who had come from Cyprus, or perhaps it was Paul himself who made the suggestion that it was time to turn elsewhere. In any event, Luke, in his characteristic vocabulary, tells us that it was under the guidance of the Holy Spirit. This first journey provides the starting point for a missionary career of Paul which carried him to thirty-two countries, over fifty cities, and many of the Mediterranean islands.

NOTES

1. Harvey Cox, *The Secular City*.

11. MEDITERRANEAN CRUISE

(Acts 13:4-49)

THE JOURNEY began from Seleucia, the seaport for Antioch and, at the time, a naval base for the eastern Mediterranean. The port of Seleucia was sixteen miles from Antioch and had—for those days—a considerable harbor. The distance from Seleucia to Salamis, on the island of Cyprus, was about one hundred fifty miles.

It is worth asking at this point why Paul and Barnabas—aside from any reasons of persuasion from Christians who had come from the place—should have chosen Cyprus as a springboard for a wider missionary endeavor than was represented by Antioch. Perhaps the answer is that the island of Cyprus had, at this time, a very Jewish population which was not only large but also influential; later on, the Jewish population led a revolt on the island of Cyprus which was mercilessly suppressed by the Ro-

man authority. Of course, there is also to be taken into
account the fact that Barnabas was a native of the island,
and, almost certainly, owned property there. (His cousin,
John Mark, may have been the author of the gospel which
bears the name Mark, though of this we cannot be certain.) Barnabas was, evidently, a person of considerable
influence in the congregations of both Jerusalem and
Antioch and it is reasonable to suggest that his influence
on Paul's early years as a Christian was equally
considerable.

Cyprus was, in Paul's day, an island of far more wealth
and influence than is the case now because, in antiquity,
it was a major source for copper (which, incidentally,
is still mined on the island). It will be of advantage to
consult an atlas which gives some indication of the
physical features of Cyprus.

After spending some time in Salamis, Paul and
Barnabas set out with John Mark westward across the
island to another seaport—Paphos, which at that time was
the capital of the island. Some fifty years before the birth
of Jesus, the Roman authorities took over the island of
Cyprus and moved the capital from Salamis to Paphos.
Those who are not well acquainted with classical history
may be a little confused by the fact that the Paphos visited
by Paul and Barnabas was ten miles away from an old
city of the same name dating back to Phoenician times.
The old Paphos had a shrine of some importance since, as
with so many other shrines in antiquity, its priests spent
most of their time answering questions through divination.
(One important visitor to this shrine was the Roman
commander, Titus, on his way to the first Jewish war
[A.D. 66 to 70]). The new city of Paphos was not
without a shrine of some importance, however. An earthquake in 15 B.C. had devastated the city and, when it
was restored under Caesar Augustus, the city was given
a new name—Augusta. For both cities, however, there

was a "presiding deity" in the person of the Greek goddess Aphrodite who, according to the classical legend, was born in the sea near Paphos. Essentially, the goddess Aphrodite, known to the Romans as Venus, was the same deity as the one known to the old Canaanite fertility rites as Astarte.

For a reason which we do not know, Paul and Barnabas were asked to speak before the resident Roman official, Sergius Paulus. He is referred to in Acts as proconsul—another indication of the accuracy with which Luke recorded the titles of dignitaries of the cities and imperial officials whom he mentions in the Acts of the Apostles. Two decades before the New Testament period Caesar Augustus removed Cyprus from his own jurisdiction to that of the Roman senate with the consequence that the supervision of the island was in the hands of a man appointed by the senate who was known as a proconsul.

We have already had something to say about Paul's Roman names. What is interesting at this point is the possibility that, since the proconsul bore the name Paulus, he may well, in some way, have been related to the apostle Paul. Not only do we have this coincidence, but we also have the coincidence of Paul preaching Jesus as Messiah and being confronted by a Jewish magus called Bar-Jesus. This man's name was really Bar-Joshua, meaning "son of Joshua" and since Joshua was a common enough name among Jews of this period, the correspondence of names is no more than of coincidental interest.

What is interesting is the strong contrast between the "Joshua" whom Paul preached as Messiah on the one hand, and the "Joshua" whom Paul encountered at Paphos as a magus. It is not easy accurately to translate this Greek word, although we can see how the words magic and magician have been derived from the Greek root. The magus encountered by Paul would have been, like so many of his contemporaries in similar occupations, an astrologer, diviner, consultant in magical potions and formulae (particularly useful when wishing to rid oneself of an enemy or an undesirable relative). The magi in New Testament times and later were often men of immense wealth, treated with very great veneration and respect by large numbers of people, and able to prey upon the fears and superstition of an age terrified of "fate" and "luck." It would be very easy to describe such men as the spiritual directors or even confessors of their time, and, in some respects, this may be the nearest approach in Christian terms to their occupation in the sense that folk resorted to them for advice and counsel. There the comparison ends because the magi operated upon a whole series of presuppositions which neither the orthodox Jew nor the Christian of St. Paul's day could possibly have accepted. The fact that this "son of Joshua" was by birth a Jew is an indication of how far he had fallen from the faith of his fathers by trafficking even in a small way in this kind of occupation. The bitterness of his reaction to the proconsul's conversion to Christianity comes alive to us in Luke's narrative, and Paul, both as Jew and Christian, is represented to us by Luke as reacting with utter loathing and distaste for the man's chosen occupation.

There now comes a very subtle shift in Luke's writing of the account. Previously, Barnabas was always mentioned first as the principal evangelist in this team of Christians, but, as soon as the party leaves Paphos, Luke introduces us to a new way of looking at things— "Paul and his companions." It is here, too, that Luke changes from Paul's Jewish name, Saul, to the Roman name, Paul. It is impossible to determine the reason for this shift in name and it is not entirely convincing to suggest, as is sometimes done, that up to this point Paul had confined his teaching to Jewish synagogues—and, therefore, Luke used the name Saul—but that after the conversion of Sergius Paulus the attentions of the apostles were directed beyond the synagogue to the larger Roman world. We are certainly correct in reading Luke's account of Paul's subsequent journeys as indicating that Paul always sought out synagogue congregations or Jewish families when first he went to a strange town. It is true, however, that Luke is always interested in the reactions of Roman authority to the new faith, and perhaps this change of name may have something to do with Paul's subsequent encounters with the Roman imperial administration in the later chapters of Acts.

The next part of the account of Paul's first missionary journey is in highly compressed form. Luke informs us that the company set sail from Paphos and went to Perga. Since this town is about ten miles inland, it may be presumed that they landed at Attalia. Perga, perched upon a fairly isolated hilltop, was a city with the streets on the usual grid pattern and some quite substantial public buildings and possessed a sports arena and a theatre of some size. The presiding deity of Perga was the goddess Artemis whom we shall meet later at Ephesus. It is at this point that Luke tells us that John Mark left Paul and Barnabas and returned to Jerusalem. He gives no reason for John Mark's departure.

Paul and Barnabas then passed from Perga to Antioch of Pisidia. It is difficult to overestimate the physical difficulties posed by this particular journey. The two companions had now left the low-lying coast land and journeyed into the interior mountain ranges of Asia Minor. The southern most part of this mountain mass was—and is—known as the Taurus range. This range can be compared reasonably with parts of the Rocky Mountains. While there were several passes going through these high mountains, they were all very narrow and incapable of taking any kind of wagon traffic. Instead, they had to be traversed either on foot or on mule back. At the very least, the journey described so tersely by Luke would have been close to 200 miles. Almost certainly, it is with this kind of journey in mind that Paul tells us of the dangers of his traveling days in his second letter to Corinth.[1] Once through this wild and inhospitable mountain range, the two companions could descend, on the northern side, to the plateau of Anatolia. Here again, if we are looking for comparisons with our own country, we can compare this plateau with the high desert of eastern Oregon. There was an infinite variety of desert, fertile valleys, and (as is true of eastern Oregon) some irrigated land.

Antioch of Pisidia was the headquarters for the administration of six Roman colonies which had been planted there in order to exercise some kind of control over the tribesmen of Anatolia. In previous generations, these very ferocious tribesmen had been a source of considerable difficulty both to the Persians and to the Greeks. It is worth noting that a colony (the Latin word is *colonia*) was a very distinctive kind of settlement and was not particularly common in the eastern part of the Roman empire. Citizens of these colonies had the same rights and privileges as citizens of Rome itself. At the time of which we are writing, Antioch in Pisidia had a very mixed population—Greeks, Anatolians, and a Jewish settlement. The city itself was considered to be a very beautiful one and contained some of the finest examples of Roman architecture in the empire. The Romans made Antioch the capital of a district known as a *regio* and it was, effectively, the center of the southern part of the whole province of Galatia.

On the first Sabbath of their arrival, Paul and Barnabas went to the synagogue in Antioch. Jews in this area had been granted all the privileges of citizenship under the Hellenistic conquest and it is probable that the same kind of privileges had been extended by the Romans when they conquered the Greek dominions. Jews seem to have achieved considerable prominence in Asia Minor as businessmen and bankers.

Paul and Barnabas on this first visit to the synagogue in Antioch were invited to address the worshipers. While this kind of invitation seems commonly to have been extended to strangers, in this particular instance it is noteworthy that Luke uses the opportunity to present us with an outline of Paul's address. The address was delivered to a congregation which will have been not unlike any other synagogue congregation of its time in that it consisted of Jews and Godfearers, who were content to remain on the outside fringes of Judaism.

This address by Paul, reproduced by Luke, differs little in content from the "typical" addresses which were recorded earlier in Acts as having been delivered by Peter.[2] In common with those early addresses of Peter, and with what has come to be called the speech of Stephen in Acts Chapter 7, the apostle Paul gave a resume of the spiritual pilgrimage of the people of Israel. Like the addresses attributed to Peter, Paul's sermon ends with a call to repentance. The record of Luke tells us that, after the congregation dispersed, many Jews and Godfearers attached themselves to Paul and Barnabas who urged them to persevere in God's grace. This sounds like an auspicious beginning but it was followed the next week by a scene only too familiar to Paul in his later travels.

On the next Sabbath day, what Luke describes as "almost the whole city" came to hear Paul and Barnabas. This large gathering of people infuriated some Jews who were not attracted to the content of Paul's message and they succeeded in creating a fairly considerable disturbance. It is at this point that Paul and Barnabas are recorded as saying that it was necessary that God's word should come to the Jews first, but that since the Jews had proved themselves unworthy of accepting the proclamation of God's act in Jesus, then they, Paul and Barnabas, would "turn to the Gentiles."

It is often suggested not only that this was a turning point in the missionary work of Paul, but that in all subsequent missionary endeavor Paul's deliberate choice of audience was Gentile rather than Jewish. This interpretation needs to be fairly heavily qualified. It is, for example, necessary only to read Paul's letters (especially Romans and the two Corinthian letters)[3] to discover how large a knowledge of the Old Testament background is demanded by Paul of his hearers. Moreover, it is recorded of Paul that on subsequent journeys he deliberately sought out his fellow Jews in the places he visited and spoke to them first. It would seem from the historical and archaeological evidence already existing that in all the places where Paul went there was already a substantial Jewish population to whose history Paul could appeal as common ground. It is likely that the majority of Paul's converts were Jews and Godfearers who stood on the fringes of the synagogue without formally committing themselves to Judaism by circumcision. I do not believe that the content of Paul's letters will bear the suggestion that Paul's proclamation of the gospel was made, initially at any rate, to pagans who hitherto had no contact with Hebrew life and thought. There is one exception to this —Paul's address to the men of Athens[4]—but that seems clearly to be regarded by Luke as an exception rather than a rule.

NOTES

1. II Corinthians 11   2. Acts 2:14-36; Acts 3:12-26   3. *e.g.* Romans 9-11   4. Acts 17:22-31.

12. CIVIL DISORDERS

(Acts 13:50-52; 14)

WHATEVER THE background of those who listened eagerly
to Paul in Antioch, the opposition to his message from
sections of the Jewish population was such that Paul
and Barnabas were driven from the city. They went
next to another important city, Iconium. Iconium was
a complete contrast to Antioch. It was not a natural
military outpost; indeed, its position on an open plain
was such that it could not easily be defended. It was,
nevertheless, an important agricultural center with a very
heavy emphasis on commerce and trading. Here again,
there was a large Jewish population. Even though the
majority of the inhabitants of the city were Phrygians,
Paul and Barnabas seem to have met with a far warmer
reception in Iconium than in Antioch, since we are told
that Paul remained there for a considerable period boldly
proclaiming the gospel. In the view of some scholars,
the evangelists spent the first winter of their journey in
Iconium. The time of enthusiastic reception was termi-
nated by the turbulence and unrest which was never far
below the surface in a Hellenistic city and Paul and
Barnabas left the city to avoid the danger of injury or
death.

After leaving Iconium, Paul and Barnabas spent one
day in travel to a small town named Lystra, a town
which was the farthest east of the six colonies in south
Galatia. It was here, on beginning to proclaim the
message of the gospel, that Paul healed a man who had
been crippled from birth. In contrast with their experience
in Iconium, the two missionaries were surrounded by an
ecstatic and enthusiastic crowd who proclaimed that this
miracle of healing was nothing less than a direct inter-

vention by the gods. Barnabas was named Zeus (the father of the gods) and Paul they named Hermes (because, as principal speaker, he was evidently the messenger of the gods). The background of this story seems to be a legend preserved by one of the Roman poets that Zeus and Hermes once came to this area disguised as men and were refused hospitality except by one poor family. The family which gave hospitality to the gods was showered with all kinds of blessings. This time, the inhabitants of Lystra did not wish to risk for the future any inability to recognize the two gods Zeus and Hermes. So enthusiastic was the crowd, that the pagan temple priests were making due preparations to offer animal sacrifices to Paul and Barnabas and only with difficulty were they restrained from proceeding with the sacrifice.

It is of incidental interest to remember that the language of this region (Lycaonian) may go back as far as a thousand years before the ministry of Jesus. Lycaonian was still in some use in the 4th century after the events of which we are speaking which may give some indication of the very isolated character of this small city.

If ever an example is needed as to the way in which enthusiasm can be channeled from one object to another in a remarkably short space of time, we have that example in the treatment accorded to Paul and Barnabas following this initial missionary endeavor in Lystra. Jews from Antioch and Iconium arrived in the city—having discovered what Paul's destination was to be—and created enough dissension and turmoil among the people to induce them to stone Paul and Barnabas. Paul was knocked out and left for dead. When his friends gathered round him and discovered that he was still alive, he was taken back into the city and on the next day he left Lystra for Derbe with Barnabas.

Derbe was a taxation center on the frontier of the province of Galatia. It was situated on a trade route from the Taurus mountains going north, as well as on another trade route which crossed the high ground of Asia Minor to the west. It was in Derbe, after Paul recovered from the mob violence in Lystra, that he and Barnabas proclaimed the gospel and made many converts. One convert (Gaius, who is referred to in Acts 20, verse 4) even accompanied Paul from Corinth into Macedonia.

It comes to us as a shock to realize that, in spite of the treatment which he and Barnabas had received in Iconium and Lystra, Paul retraced his steps to Lystra, Iconium, and Antioch. It is possible that those who initiated the riotous disturbances had left Iconium and Lystra, or that Paul and Barnabas returned to those towns unobserved and made contact with the disciples privately. It may also be that Paul invoked his Roman citizenship to protect him from mob violence but of this we cannot be certain. If he did, indeed, make full use of the privileges of Roman citizenship, then there would have been great hesitation on the part of any mob to attack a Roman citizen who was uncondemned. It has been conjectured that Paul carried with him some proof of his citizenship and there is some evidence for the use of a kind of birth certificate in the period after Paul's missionary activities. It is known that a complete list was kept in the city of Rome of all citizens of Rome, together with certain records of family descent and affiliation. About the time of the apostle Paul, the number of citizens was around six million.

It is very difficult in our reading of the New Testament records in the Acts of the Apostles to discover exactly where the line was drawn between missionary preaching on the one hand and the necessity of providing for organized life in the Christian communities on the other. It seems to be the case that on the first journey through the cities of Galatia, Paul and Barnabas had confined their work almost exclusively to teaching and preaching. However, it must not be supposed that Paul the Jew and Paul the Christian were two entirely different kinds of person. Paul, as a good Pharisee, would behave as sensitively to the necessity of good organization as would any other Jew. Paul would have been the very last person to suppose that enthusiasm would sustain for any indefinite period the faith and the devotion of those newly converted to Christianity. Furthermore, if the suggestions made at the beginning of this book have any validity, then we may suppose that the kind of organizational pattern which was established early in Jerusalem may well have accompanied Paul and Barnabas on their evangelizing missions over the Mediterranean. In any event, the return visits to the cities of Galatia seem to have been employed by Paul and Barnabas in strengthening the pattern of community life in each local church. While we do not know with any certainty when these Pauline congregations began permanently to withdraw from any association with Judaism or the synagogue, we do know, for example, that many Christians, and certainly Jewish Christians, found themselves, in the period after the First Jewish War (A.D. 66-70), torn in their loyalties. The nationalist Jewish groups had a perfect right to ask how far a new-found messianic faith made any difference to the Jewish loyalties of the convert, while the Roman imperial authority might be excused for regarding all Jews—and fringe-sectarians such as Christians—as alike enemies of the state. But if—as some scholars suppose—the majority of Paul's converts were, in fact, Gentiles, then the breach between Christianity and Judaism in Paul's congregations may well have been quite early. The author believes that this view is much too simple. In the absence of evidence, it is unwise to be too definite about what did or did not happen in the congregations for which Paul was initially responsible.

It is certain, however, that the parts of the Roman Empire evangelized by Paul all assumed a common stamp and took on, in all essential characteristics, the same mold as each other. We may regard it as providential that this early evangelism was conducted by one man, for in that way Christians could realize and recognize their essential unity with each other if and when they went from one local congregation or church to another.

On the way home, Paul and Barnabas stopped in Perga in order to preach and teach there and then sailed from Attalia back home to Antioch in Syria. On their arrival home, they assembled the Christians in Antioch and gave an account of their missionary endeavors.

13. A QUESTION OF DISCRIMINATION

(Acts 15:1-35)

IF THERE is one area of debate which is particularly tantalizing about Paul's relationship with the Church in Jerusalem, it is the question of what was, or was not, accomplished at the meeting in Jerusalem which is related in Acts, Chapter 15. This meeting has been described in many books as a council, inferring that it possessed some kind of overriding authority over the activities of Christian missionaries, including Paul. The real difficulty with this view is that—whatever was accomplished or discussed at Jerusalem—Paul does not regard this meeting as of definitive importance, nor, in his later writings, does he appear to refer to it as being binding in any sense. To this question we shall return later in an appendix.

It was at home in Antioch that Paul and Barnabas found themselves faced with a very serious threat to their freedom in proclaiming the gospel to Gentiles. Apparently, some had come from Judaea and were busily engaged in teaching the Christians that unless they were circumcised according to the law of Moses they could not be accepted into the community of the Gospel. The situation was regarded as so serious that Paul and Barnabas, together with some others, were appointed by the congregation in Antioch to go to Jerusalem about this matter. On arrival there, they were welcomed by the Jerusalem congregation and the apostles, who related all that had occurred in their missionary journeys. There were some who having previously been Pharisees, took the same line about Paul's missionary activities as was taken by the critics who had gone from Jerusalem to Antioch.

It is very difficult to have any kind of real sympathy for Paul's critics at this point. However, it is very important for us to attempt to see what was being said by them. So far as our New Testament records go, it seems to have been Paul who first realized that any assertion that God, in Jesus, had made it possible for men to enter into a new relationship with God through the remission of sin must carry with it the inevitable consequence that such a forgiveness and such a new relationship was of universal applicability. There are two things, here, which we must bear in mind. The first is the question, written large across the pages of the Old Testament, "If God hates sin, then how can he possibly forgive it?" It is not easily remembered by us that the Old Testament knows no forgiveness for what is called "high-handed"—or deliberate—sin. Secondly, Paul's critics could well claim that only the Jew was expecting a decisive intervention by God in the field of human history. It was only the Jew who had talked, thought, and prayed in terms of an Anointed Servant of God who would not only announce but also establish God's visible reign

among men. It must, therefore, have come as a considerable, or even bitter, surprise to Paul's Jewish critics to
find that they themselves might very soon become a
minority in what, in their view, was a legitimate messianic
party within or on the fringes of Judaism. The whole
question, therefore, of the allegiance of these new converts
to the law of Moses was, to Paul's critics, of enormous
importance. After all, if expressions like "Messiah" or
"Kingdom of God" or "new covenant" had any validity
at all, they had their first validity within the confines of
Judaism. Paul's critics, therefore, maintained—and if we
are sympathetic, we shall try to see their point of view—
that it was necessary for those who came to faith in
Jesus as Messiah first to submit themselves to that
covenant community to which alone the Messiah had
been first promised.

As we see when we look at Paul's letters, any
compromise with the universality of the gospel was to
Paul an outrage. For Paul, sin was a universal human
condition and if God had offered to men, even though
first of all through the covenant community of Judaism,
the possibility of forgiveness of sin through the Gospel,
then such forgiveness must apply to all men regardless of
ethnic origin. We do not know how the debate raged
or into what areas it ranged, but it is perfectly possible
that some of Paul's critics may well have reminded him
that, in the pagan world in which they lived, it was only
the Jew who regarded sin with any seriousness as willed
rebellion against God.

It was the apostle Peter who reminded those who
met in Jerusalem that it was through his own mission
to Cornelius[1] that the gentiles first heard the gospel and
had been accepted into the community of believers on
the basis of faith in God's redeeming act, and not on any
basis of submission to Judaism. According to the record
left by Luke, James—who seems to have acted as president

of the gathering—later gave his decision that Gentile converts did not have to obey the Mosaic law. What follows in Acts 15:6-11 and 20 is not easy for us to interpret. The sense seems to imply that, while not under obligation to the Mosaic law, Gentile converts must, at the same time, abstain from idolatry, unchastity, and from non-kosher meat. However, it is equally possible to interpret the prohibitions contained in these verses as being more of an assertion of the provisions of the Mosaic law against blood feuds, against casual divorce and remarriage, and against eating meat whose origin was sacrificial in the pagan sense.[2]

The Jerusalem community is then reported by Luke to have composed an official letter spelling out the details of the decisions of the meeting in Jerusalem. Luke tells us that the letter was sent by the hands of Paul and Barnabas, along with other leading members of the congregation, back to Antioch.

Paul and Barnabas, with others, remained in Antioch teaching and preaching; how long they remained there is not entirely clear.

NOTES

1. Acts 10.
2. For the difficulties of chronology and interpretation of this meeting in Jerusalem, see the Appendix.

14. MORE RIOTS

(Acts 15:36-41; 16; 17:1-15)

It was Paul's suggestion, after some time in Antioch, that he and Barnabas should revisit the places where they had previously preached and taught. It was Paul's refusal to allow John Mark to join this second journey which ruptured the partnership between Paul and Barnabas. Paul chose Silas (Silvanus) to accompany him on this new enterprise. Silas is remembered as one of the persons who journeyed from Jerusalem to Antioch to convey to that congregation the decisions of the meeting in Jerusalem and must have been a man of quite outstanding ability. While he is called by his longer name—Silvanus—in the letters of both Paul and Peter,[1] it is Luke who calls him Silas, the name by which, evidently, he was known in Jerusalem. Apart from his ability to work with two such diverse characters as Peter and Paul and the fact that, like Paul, he was a Roman citizen, we know very little about Silas.

The exact nature of the relationship between Silas and the apostles Peter and Paul is very difficult to discover from our records in the New Testament. For example, if the first letter of Peter is, in any sense, a genuine product of the apostle Peter, it was Silas who first brought news to Peter of the progress of Christian congregations in the northern part of Asia Minor.[2]

The provinces mentioned in this first leter of Peter bordered on the Black Sea. The provinces so mentioned are also joined to the northern part of Galatia which was not visited in Paul's first missionary journey. Paul certainly planned to go to the southern part of the province of Asia on his second missionary journey, accompanied by Silas, but was not permitted to do so. It was on his third missionary journey that he went through this part of the world, including the vitally important city of Ephesus.

It would seem—again, if the first letter of Peter is genuinely from the apostle's own hand[3]—that after Silas disappears from our view in Luke's record, he taught and preached in the areas which Paul could not reach and then wrote or reported to the apostle Peter, wherever

Peter was at the time. Incidentally, the congregations in this part of Asia (Bythinia and Pontus) were the object of extremely savage persecution under the Emperor Trajan (A.D. 98-117).

During this second missionary journey Paul and Silas traveled overland from Antioch into Anatolia. This not only gave opportunity to revisit churches founded by Paul in the time between his leaving Jerusalem and the time when he was chosen with Barnabas as missionary by the congregation in Antioch, but also gave the two companions an opportunity to cross some of the most spectacular mountain scenery in Europe. The journey after leaving Tarsus, Paul's own home town, involved climbing through the Cilician pass through the Taurus range. The pass is about eighty miles long and—for those interested in mountain scenery—has often been described as one of the most spectacular sights in the world.

The first city mentioned in Luke's account of the journey is Derbe. Paul is reported on this occasion to have spent his time consolidating the work previously begun in Derbe.

Somewhere in this second missionary journey, another person was added to the party—Timothy. Timothy is reported by Luke to have been a young man well thought of by the congregations of both Lystra and Iconium. Timothy's mother was a Jewish Christian; his father was a Greek. Under Jewish law, Timothy was regarded as a Jew and it is this circumstance which prompted Paul to have Timothy circumcised before he joined the others as part of the evangelizing team. From time to time, writers on the New Testament have expressed bewilderment at the action of Paul in having Timothy circumcised, since this seems to be at variance with his often proclaimed position that under the Gospel there was no distinction between Jew and Gentile. But Paul was alive to the advantages of having Timothy's status as a Jew regularized since this would allow Timothy to teach and preach the Gospel in specifically Jewish congregations. Timothy later became one of Paul's most trusted workers whom he referred to as his "son." If the two New Testament letters which purport to be addressed to Timothy are genuine[4], then Paul's concern for Timothy's well being can be seen very clearly.

Luke tells us that the missionary band went through Phrygia and Galatia but that, due to circumstances upon which Luke does not elaborate, they found it impossible to go into Asia. Luke's statement is that they were "forbidden by the Holy Spirit to speak" in Asia. We are not told what circumstances compelled Paul and his companions to go to Troas, but it is interesting to speculate what the history of early Christian missionary enterprise might have been if Paul and his companions had evangelized the Black Sea area. As it was, from Antioch in Pisidia Paul and his companions reached Troas having, in the process, crossed the high country of Asia Minor from southeast to northwest.

Many of us will be familiar with the exciting story of the discovery of Troy by Schliemann.[5] The tale of that discovery and excavation does not rightly belong here but is a fascinating story in its own right with the dedicated perseverance of Schliemann and his wife being one of the absorbing tales of 19th-century exploration. Successor to ancient Troy, the city of Troas was founded about the year 300 B.C. and was taken over by the Romans in 133 B.C. The city itself was of considerable importance and there is a substantial amount of archaeological evidence to show how important this Roman colony was in the time of Paul.

At this point in Luke's narrative we are told that one night Paul, in a vision or dream, was visited by a man of Macedonia urging him to come to the people there. It is noteworthy that it is at this point in Acts,

Luke uses for the first time the description "we." It is difficult to know whether Luke is intending by the use of this term to indicate that he himself joined the party at this point or whether he is simply quoting from a "travel diary," incorporating it into the main body of his own work. Another suggestion sometimes offered is that it was Luke himself who urged upon Paul the necessity of preaching the Gospel in Macedonia. Professional New Testament scholars have argued at great length in favor of all these ideas, and there is no unanimity among them as to whether Luke was, or was not, writing from first hand experience when he uses the plural pronoun "we."

The party set sail under favorable winds from Troas and hurried on through Samothrace to the large and important Roman city of Philippi. This city was named in honor of Philip of Macedon, the father of Alexander the Great, not only because of its proximity to gold mines which had provided the wealth for Philip's conquests but also because of its situation on the boundaries of some of the finest land in Macedonia. Macedonia became part of the Roman imperial system in 168 B.C.

Luke's account tells of Paul's first missionary endeavors in Philippi among Jews who went down to the riverside for Sabbath Day prayers. It is of some interest to us that Luke records that this congregation of Jewish worshipers at Philippi consisted entirely of women. The conversion of Lydia is of outstanding importance in this episode. She is described, in the Acts of the Apostles, as a business woman of some importance, representing the purple dye industry of Thyatira. While this purple dye was certainly not of the best quality, its use being confined largely to the less affluent members of society, we know from classical sources that it had a very ready sale. We can assume, therefore, that Lydia—and the firm she represented—would find a steady source of income

among the citizens of the colony. It was not simply that
Paul gained entry through Lydia into the business
community of Philippi, there was the additional factor
that the conversion of Lydia provided a meeting place
for the first Christian converts in Philippi.

But the progress made by the conversion of Lydia
and the provision through her of a meeting place for
instruction and worship was speedily and abruptly broken
by an episode which Luke reports at length. A slave girl
was making her owners large sums of money through
her gifts of divination. Whatever Paul's attitude might
have been to something which we might call ESP or
"the sight," he very evidently regarded the exploitation
of such psychic gifts as the girl possessed as a work of
the devil. He, therefore, exorcised the slave girl and, in
so doing, brought down upon himself and Silas the
vitriolic hatred of her former owners. They brought Paul
and Silas before the examining magistrates and asserted
that, since Paul and Silas were Jews, they were beginning
to disturb the city and introducing customs which were
not lawful for Romans to accept. It is not easy to discover
exactly what the accusation meant. It is conceivable that,
although Judaism was a tolerated religion in the Roman
Empire, Jews were not allowed to proselytize Roman
citizens. Or, just possibly, the edict of the Emperor
Claudius expelling Jews from the city of Rome[6] may have
been invoked by these enraged citizens of Philippi in
order to exact vengeance on Paul. Whatever the truth of
the matter may be, the magistrates responded to a possible
outbreak of riot by having Paul and Silas flogged and
thrown into prison.

Luke's record tells us that, during a service of prayer
which Paul and Silas were holding in prison, there was
a sudden earthquake which made it possible for the
prisoners to escape. The Roman jailer, seeing the havoc
caused by the earthquake in the prison, assumed that

some of his prisoners had, in fact, escaped (for which he would be held accountable) and was about to commit suicide. Paul persuaded the jailer to give up his plan for suicide and taught the keeper of the prison the necessity for not only saving his physical life but also saving his spiritual life. The account given by Luke is somewhat confused, however. The action of the magistrates the next day, in sending to release Paul and Silas, indicates that they knew that they had acted illegally in flogging two Roman citizens. Yet, in Luke's account, when the magistrates sent to the prison the command to release Paul and Silas and urged them to leave the city, Paul's angry response that they had beaten Roman citizens illegally is met with astonishment.

The urgency of the magistrates' request that the evangelists leave the city was ignored for the time being by Paul and Silas who returned to Lydia's house to talk further with their new converts.

Paul's next stop on this road of missionary travels was in Thessalonica, forty miles from Philippi, across rich fertile valley land. The city itself was a very important harbor on the northern part of the Aegean Sea, controlling a great deal of commerce and trade and controlling, too, a good deal of territory for some miles inland. In common with most large cities in the Mediterranean, Thessalonica had a synagogue and it was here that Paul began his work. Thessalonica is interesting in that it had something approaching an elected assembly of citizens—a relic of older days under Greek domination—but now only a shadow of its former self, as well as a panel of officials whom Luke called *politarchs*.[7] It is interesting to observe that Luke's use of this term is an indication of his care as a historian, since the term itself has been confirmed by records on inscriptions of Luke's own time.

The modern city of Salonica is on the site of the Thessalonica of New Testament times. Much of the scenery around Thessalonica is dominated by Mount Olympus which was the home of the old Greek gods. We can only surmise as to whether it was the location of Thessalonica so near to Mt. Olympus that prompted Paul to begin storming the fortress of Greek paganism. In any event, it was in Thessalonica that Paul found for himself a new companion in missionary enterprise named Aristarchus who remained with him to the end of the story as Luke tells it.[8] It was in this city, according to Luke, that Paul converted some Jews and many Greeks, including some prominent women. Biblical scholars have long noted that both Luke's gospel and the Acts of the Apostles give a very prominent place to women. It is, therefore, interesting to see at this point that, apparently, women were accustomed to much more esteem in Macedonia than almost anywhere else in the Greek-dominated Mediterranean.

Paul's missionary work, here as elsewhere, provoked a storm of criticism and aroused the anger of the mob. In this instance, Paul and his companions, living in a house belonging to a man called Jason, were dragged from the house by the mob and brought before the civic authorities. The charge against them was that they had "turned the world upside down"—and, more interesting than this, they were proclaiming an emperor other than Caesar. The city authorities who were very quick to realize that they might very easily have a full-scale riot on their hands, with great promptitude—though certainly illegally—expelled Paul and Silas from the city.

Paul and Silas went away by night from Thessalonica to the southwest to Beroea. In contrast with what had happened in Thessalonica, Luke writes that the Jews in Beroea received Paul's message with enthusiasm and spent their time examining the Hebrew scriptures to see how valid Paul's message was over against their own expectations. Luke goes on to say that Paul's teaching converted many Jews together with some prominent Greek women. This work was impeded, once more, by Jews from Thessalonica who arrived on the scene and stirred up trouble for the apostle. In the end, Silas and Timothy remained behind with this new group of Christians, while Paul himself went on to Athens escorted by some members of the congregation in Beroea.

NOTES

1. II Corinthians 1:19. I Peter 5:12.
2. I Peter 5:12.
3. This writer is strongly of the opinion that this first letter may well represent the thought of Peter as mediated through the mind and pen of a secretary. Far too little attention is given to the part played by such people in the letters of Peter and Paul in our existing books.
4. Recent New Testament writing has been far more reluctant than was the case some years ago in dismissing the letters to Timothy as non-Pauline. For one thing, it is no longer wholly adequate to dismiss the letters on the ground that they betray a concern for church organization which was characteristic only of a later age. In fact, there are almost no common features between the kind of organization assumed by the two letters and, for example, the letters of Ignatius of Antioch (c. 110).
5. Heinrich Schliemann, who excavated the site of ancient Troy in the 1870's.
6. 49 A.D.
7. Acts 17:16 "magistrates"—New English Bible, "city council"—Jerusalem Bible.
8. See Acts 20:4.

15. MEN OF ATHENS

(Acts 17:16-34)

IN SPITE of the fact that it was only a city—the center of one city-state among many others—the name Athens is associated in the minds of most people with the whole of mainland Greece. When Paul arrived in Athens, many of the glorious temples and buildings were still standing, and the Acropolis was the crowning architectural glory of an extremely beautiful city.

In many ways, however, the intellectual status of Athens had changed drastically since the days of the great philosophers Socrates, Plato, and Aristotle. Athens had become, by the time St. Paul visited it, one center of learning among many others, its former academic glory, in some ways, having been overshadowed by Alexandria. Nevertheless, Roman citizens who had the means to do so generally insisted that their sons go to Athens to study. If the intellectual climate of Athens had changed it was in ways which were not immediately appreciated. The great philosophers, particularly Socrates, had put the process of rational thinking within the reach of ordinary men and women by what has come to be called the "Socratic method." It was Socrates who had taught men to question their assumptions and presuppositions in ordinary thinking and subject them to close scrutiny. It was Socrates and Plato who had insisted that men and women examine the rules by which they argued cases and the grounds upon which they held their presuppositions. One of the results of this questioning had been a very serious erosion of any kind of intellectual content attaching to the old Greek religious myths. In fact, it was hardly possible in the century in which Paul taught for any intelligent man or woman to give serious credence to the previously unquestioned assumptions of Greek religion. Certainly, the old Greek gods and goddesses had long since ceased to be credible and, if they were worshiped at all, that worship was the perfunctory performance of a civic duty.

What had largely taken the place of the old religious observances, or at any rate among intelligent people, was the pursuit of the philosophical disciplines of the Stoics. It would be very difficult, in the space of a short sentence or two, to describe accurately the main tenets of Stoic philosophy and there would be very grave risk of serious misunderstanding if such an attempt was made. Perhaps the closest we can come to summing up the Stoic approach to life is to say that Stoic philosophy in general taught an acceptance of the world in which men lived, the circumstances within which their lives were lived out, and, over it all, a strong sense of moral duty and obligation to family, friends, and civic society.

Although the customary religious observances still went on, they were largely devoid of genuine content, except perhaps among simpler people, and Paul's missionary methods in Athens, interestingly, were different from what we might have expected. Luke's account of Paul's preaching and teaching in Athens contains no massive onslaught by Paul against the pagan gods. Indeed, Luke represents Paul as ignoring the old religion and going first, as he always did, to Jews and Godfearers whom he happened to meet. However, the atmosphere of Athens was such that there was a great deal of curiosity, some serious, some merely cursory, about any manifestation of new items of inquiry or new systems of teaching. Luke's description of this intellectual climate is entirely accurate.

Paul, then, left to one side as of no importance the old religion and concentrated instead upon the intellectuals whom he met in the public places where philosophical discussions were usually carried on. It is very difficult to assess how far Luke's account of Paul's address to the intellectuals of Athens in Acts 17 is an accurate piece of historical reporting, or whether it represents Luke's own attempt at giving in microcosm the kind of approach that Paul made to Greek intellectuals when he chanced upon them. There is nothing inherently improbable in Luke's having received an account of Paul's teaching in Athens from the apostle himself and there is an appropriateness about Paul's address as coming from a devout Jewish Christian who, at the same time, was well acquainted with the way in which Greek secular thinking was evolving in his own time. The slow death of the old religion, save as providing occasions for public holidays, had left an enormous void in Greek life on the religious level. The encounter of the apostle with an altar which had an inscription "to an unknown God" accurately represents the emptiness of the religious scene as Paul knew it in Hellenistic society.

Paul, in his address to the intellectuals in Athens, emphasized—as any Jewish Christian would—God's action as Creator. But Paul's next theme, if this is an accurate representation of his teaching to Greek audiences, must have provided more than a little bewilderment to many of his hearers. Paul next propounded the theological presupposition which underlies all Old Testament thought —that of God's overarching concern for his creation and for the human race which inhabits this planet. Paul's words as they stand in this account of his address are obviously diametrically opposed to any notion that a man must simply *accept* the universe and his fellowmen. The Christian virtue of faithful response to the Creator carries with it an obligation to attempt to discover the divine will both for the world and for oneself. To the Stoic philosopher, such a quest would have seemed a very odd way of responding to the situation in which men were placed by birth or in which they found themselves by all the forces of education, environment, and upbringing. Perhaps, one of the things which led to a slow death of the Greek gods and the loosening of their hold on men's imagination and piety was the totally capricious and only too human, and sometimes inhuman, behavior of the gods themselves in Greek myth and legend. It is extremely difficult in reading the Greek myths to find any way in which one could accommodate a notion of "providence" to the old gods of Olympus.

Paul's next concern in his address was with the matter of "redemption." The idea that God would come to the rescue of men, especially of his people Israel, was common enough in the Old Testament and the word "redemption" was one way in which God's vindication of his people would be accomplished. For Paul, God's definitive and final act of redemption had been accomplished through his expected Messianic deliverer, Jesus. But Paul introduced the matter of redemption into his address by a quotation from Stoic philosophy—"for we are truly his offspring." Paul challenged his hearers with this text from the poet Cleanthes.[1] The force of Paul's argument was based on God as person. Paul reminded his audience that, if, indeed, we are the creation of God, then to make God less than ourselves—that is to say, make God less than personal—is to detract from the Godhead. If, therefore, God is supremely personal, and our own personhood a pale reflection of person as it is in God, then we have no right to suppose that God can be, or will be, indifferent to human sin and rebellion. Paul concluded this part of his address with an appeal to repentance.

It is hard to imagine the reactions of his audience to this appeal. After all, Paul, for all his Hellenism, was a Jewish Christian to whom the idea of sin as deliberate, willed rebellion against God was commonplace. Indeed, when Paul writes later on to the Christians in Rome, he is careful to use the word "rebellion" as part of his vocabulary in dealing with the notion of sin. But for the educated Greek of his own day, the idea of sin as a conscious rebellion against an all-holy, personal God was not only foreign, but also may have been quite distasteful. To the majority of Greeks sin was almost an accidental "missing the mark." In fact, the most common word for sin in our Greek New Testament is a word which derives from archery and was used to describe missing a target. It is easy to see how that kind of notion could carry with it, for many people, the fatal misunderstanding that sin is in some way or other inherent in human nature as God created it. Paul's appeal, on the other hand, is based on a precisely opposite premise—that God created man for union with himself and that sin was not inherently part of creation as God intended it.

Whatever the reactions of his audience might have been to Paul's call to repentance, the greatest controversy arose when Paul came to deal with the Resurrection. A great many people were astounded; some laughed at Paul and at the whole idea of resurrection. Perhaps there was an air of faint condescension towards this educated Jew who was asking an audience of sophisticated Greeks to believe that God's purpose for mankind had been declared through a Jew who had died a shameful death, even though he was raised from the dead.

It has occasionally been said by writers on the New Testament that this kind of sermon or address by Paul represented a solitary excursion into this sort of appeal to an educated audience. It is often said that Paul saw the hopelessness of this appeal and in future missionary enterprises abandoned it altogether. Such judgments overlook the fact that when Paul wrote to Christians in Rome he opened his letter by a very extended treatment of the kind of themes which are to be found in his address in Athens.

NOTES

1. Also ascribed to a Cilician poet, Anatus in *Phaenomene.*

16. THROWN OUT OF COURT

(Acts 18:1-22)

ONE OF the most important pieces of missionary work undertaken by Paul was in the city of Corinth. Not only was his work there important and not only was it evident that he expended a considerable amount of energy in building the Christian congregation there, it is also the case that the two letters which survive in our New Testament addressed to the Corinthian church touch on a whole series of extremely important questions of which we might otherwise have known very little.

The physical situation of Corinth made it the important city that it was in the days of the apostle. A narrow strip of land, an isthmus—at its narrowest only four miles wide—is the connecting land link between the northern and the southern parts of Greece. Obviously, all trade going north and south was channeled through this narrow strip of land. The southern peninsula of Greece was, and is, visited frequently by very severe storms, and its coastline provided the scene of many shipwrecks. The devastation which might have been caused to trade and commerce through loss of shipping was avoided by the sheltered character of the Gulf of Corinth. Corinth itself is at almost the narrowest point of the isthmus.

Since the isthmus was so narrow at this point there was, in antiquity, an ingenious road along which smaller ships could be transported on rollers and flatbed-wagons from Corinth to the Aegean Sea. Larger ships simply unloaded their cargo which was conveyed by the same method across the isthmus by road, sections of which have been uncovered by archaeologists. On this narrow isthmus there was a port on the west and another on the east, with Corinth itself farther toward the western side but about two miles south of the road between the two ports. The Emperor Nero, a short time before his death, commissioned the Roman equivalent of the corps of engineers to cut a canal through the isthmus to join the two seas. This project was abandoned after Nero's death, and the long-projected canal was not completed until the closing years of the 19th century.

For all of its importance in antiquity, Corinth had been destroyed by the conquering Romans in the second century B.C. and its rebuilding was not begun until 44 B.C. At its rebuilding, Corinth became a "colony." This was a technical term under Roman law, the nearest equivalent in modern American history being the deliberate settlement of the West under the federal homesteading acts of the 19th century. Those who came to the Corinthian colony were Roman veterans, freedmen (which meant, largely, freed prisoners of war), and slaves who had been given their freedom.

It will be obvious, from what has been said—and even more from a glance at a map—that Corinth became, inevitably, a very important center of trade and a bustling cosmopolitan settlement. Natives of all the countries bordering on the Mediterranean were to be found in Corinth and as a commercial center it was almost as important as Antioch in Syria. But the kind of reputation which Corinth has achieved through the glimpses we have of Corinthians in Paul's letters was a reputation which reached back into antiquity. The cosmopolitan character of Corinth, its bustling activity, its mingling of cultures, its "melting-pot" character as a meeting place for all races, gave rise to the multiplicity of problems associated with such an area. The notoriety of many Corinthian women for sexual promiscuity was well known to antiquity and Paul seems to have found part of that character little changed in his own day!

It is very easy to condemn the Corinthians for their factions, for their unbridled passion for good things, for their easy acceptance of sexual immorality, and for their greed.[1] There can be few preachers who have not, at one time or another, used the example of Corinth as a symbol for wickedness in all of its manifestations. It is important, however, to try to be sympathetic. Not only, as has been indicated, were the old religious values, for what they were worth, being steadily eroded throughout the Hellenistic world, but the very nature of the commercial activity of Corinth gave very little opportunity for the kind of academic and philosophical reflection which remained characteristic of Athens. Moreover, Corinth was a city through which thousands of travelers passed on their way from one place to another. A moment's reflection ought to persuade us that the supreme miracle of Corinth is that it was possible to establish a Christian congregation there at all. For all the trouble which it gave to the apostle Paul, the members of the Christian congregation in Corinth were, very plainly, dear to his heart. It is not possible to imagine a pastor spending the time and the energy which Paul expended on his Corinthian converts without at the same time acknowledging that the time so spent was freely given to people for whom the pastor had a great deal of affection.

The kinds of topics which Paul discusses in his first letter to Corinth—women wearing veils in church(?), the question of whether or not to buy meat sold in the ordinary butcher shops,[2] behavior at the Eucharist and at community meals, the subject of resurrection from the dead—are all matters which, in one way or another, are still in some part subjects of concern among us today.

Luke tells us that, in accordance with his usual prac-

tice, Paul began his teaching work in the Jewish synagogue. Here, as in other places, there was considerable
bitterness on the part of some Jews against Paul and it
was in Corinth that Paul made his famous statement:
"From this time onwards I will go to the Gentiles." Because the president of the synagogue, Crispus, and a number of other Corinthians eventually were baptized, it is
important not to exaggerate this "turn to the Gentiles"
of St. Paul. This was not a radical departure in the sense
that from this time on his mission would be exclusively
devoted to Gentiles; he probably wished to indicate that,
in the face of opposition, he felt free to seek an entrance
for teaching the gospel at any place where that entrance
could be found. In practice, however, Paul's missionary
custom remained the same—he appealed at first, and
wherever possible, to those whose background predis-
posed them to listen to a message about the promised
Messiah.

It was in Corinth that Paul was upheld and encour-
aged by a vision in his determination to proceed in his
endeavors. We have already referred to the subject of
visions and, whatever form this encouragement took, it
gives us an interesting insight into the intense depression
which Paul must often have suffered in the course of his
missionary work.

Jewish opposition to Paul in Corinth led eventually
to his being brought before the proconsul of Achaia,
Gallio. Unlike others mentioned in Acts, we know quite
a lot about Gallio. He is referred to by two Roman historians and was the brother of the philosopher Seneca
who was a tutor to the Emperor Nero when Nero was a
young man. The accusation against Paul was that he was
encouraging men to worship God "contrary to the law."
Gallio's response to this charge by the Jews was short
tempered and probably unexpected. He refused to be a
judge in matters which concerned loyalty to the Jewish

law. He resolutely refused to be involved in questions which appeared to him to have more to do with the interior polity of Judaism than with loyalty to the Roman state. Gallio was so unconcerned about this that, when a mob attacked the president of the synagogue and beat him in front of Gallio's own judicial bench, he was not disposed to interfere.

It has sometimes been suggested that one of the reasons that prompted Luke to write the Acts of the Apostles was to demonstrate that Christianity, as springing from Judaism, was a tolerated religious practice. That is to say, in terms of Roman law, Christianity was a *religio licita*.[3] Whether or not this was one of the reasons which prompted Luke to write so extensively about the ministry of Paul or not, the action of Gallio would seem to have established a precedent in his own province at any rate.

It was in Corinth that Paul came into contact with Aquila, a tent-maker, and Priscilla. Tentmaking may occur to us as not being the sort of thing we associate with "big business." However, the huge crowds attending the games every two years demanded tent accommodation on a very extensive scale and the type of tentmaking which went on in this part of the world included making shelters for the market place. It is also possible that the team which Paul used in his missionary campaigns may also have been engaged in sailmaking.

Paul appears to have been teaching and looking after his Christians in Corinth for at least eighteen months before he sailed for Syria with Priscilla and Aquila.[4]

The little party arrived in Ephesus and Paul himself went to the synagogue to talk to the Jews there. He was asked to stay longer but declined promising he would return later. We shall be thinking of Ephesus in the next chapter since it was on his third missionary journey that Paul stayed for three years in that city.

No account is given in Acts of the journey from Ephesus to Caesarea in Palestine. From Caesarea, Paul went to Jerusalem, presumably to give an account of his mission, and then went on to Antioch which was the base from which his missionary endeavors began.

NOTES

1. See I Corinthians 5, for example.

2. The real difficulty of meat bought in the butchers' shops was that most of it had been sprinkled with lustral water from pagan temples, or had been blessed by pagan priests. Christians responded to the situation either with contempt (the pagan gods were "nobodies") or with conscientious abstention from anything associated with paganism. Paul had to spend a great deal of time over this problem. For us, the real question is: To what extent must we always defer to the conscientious scruples of other people? Again, it was the accepted custom in many places in Greek society for only a prostitute to go without a veil—and presumably some of Paul's converts were of that class of woman and would be easily identifiable in a congregation. What concern is a man's livelihood to the rest of his fellow-Christians? Are there occupations which are totally unfitting for a Christian?

3. In Roman law, a *religio licita* was a tolerated religious practice which exempted a person from participation in city and state (pagan) festivals and which also exempted from participation in the (later) developed imperial cultus. Though primarily an exemption granted to Jews, it would have been claimed (initially, at any rate) by Christians. Unhappily, though we know of the existence of the law, we do not have any information about its date.

4. See Numbers 6:1-21. Before leaving for Syria, Paul is recorded by Luke to have "cut his hair because of a vow." Occasionally, Christian commentators on the Acts of the Apostles express bewilderment about this apparent inconsistency in Paul's conduct. They sometimes inquire as to how it came about that the apostle could insist that the Law of Moses (at any rate in its ritual prescription) was not of obligation upon Christians and then, as in this instance, apparently revert to his Pharisaic Judaism. It needs to be pointed out that at no time did Paul express any emancipation *for himself* from the prescriptions of the Mosaic Law although he does appear to have given considerable freedom and latitude to Jews who embraced the

Christian faith. Paul's strongest insistence in his letters is that the Law of Moses doesn't, and can't apply to *Gentiles* who became Christians. In the example before us, it is possible that Paul bound himself voluntarily by the vow of the Nazirite to give thanks to God for a special blessing.

17. ROUSED TO FURY

(Acts 18:23 — 21:17)

PAUL'S THIRD missionary journey, from approximately 53 A.D. to 59 A.D., covered a good deal of territory, starting from Antioch. Leaving there, we are told by Luke in a remarkable compression, Paul went from place to place through Galatia, through the "upper country," and on to Ephesus. This journey is condensed into two or three verses of text by Luke.

We know a great deal about Ephesus, both from the point of view of history and politics, and, in more recent years, archeology. It was the capital of the Roman province of Asia and, politically, the third most important city in the Roman Empire. Originally, Ephesus had been a colony from Athens and, situated as it was at the mouth of a river, now dried up, it achieved much of its importance from commerce from various parts of the province. It is possible that by the time Paul visited Ephesus it numbered around two hundred thousand inhabitants.

Even the condensed account by Luke gives us an indication of the importance of Ephesus as a "shrine city." For all the Greek dress which the city wore, its importance as a shrine was Greek in name only. Although the goddess of Ephesus was called Artemis,[1] her ancestry was much older and the temple officials were not Greek. For example, the chief priest of Artemis was an Anatolian. Most of the priestesses attached to the shrine were prostitutes, somewhat similar to those of the goddess Aphrodite in Corinth. There was nothing Greek about the representations of Artemis in statuary and very little to remind one of the hunting goddess to be found in other parts of the Greek world. The representations which are known to us from Ephesus of the goddess Artemis take us back to Minoan civilization with its representation of a many-breasted fertility goddess.

The sanctuary of Artemis at Ephesus was of very great importance and successive temples to the goddess, dating back to the eighth century B.C., were all of them of considerable architectural pretensions. The temple erected in the time of Alexander the Great was four times as large as the Parthenon at Athens and was considered to be one of the seven wonders of the ancient world.[2] In later days, the imperial cult of Rome and the emperor arrived in Ephesus and achieved importance there because of the political importance of the city itself.

On his second missionary journey, Paul had visited Ephesus very briefly, his work being cut short by the necessity of his having to return to Jerusalem and Antioch. On his third missionary journey he returned to Ephesus and remained for a period of three years. In spite of the fact that he was there for the longest stay in any one city throughout his ministry, only the highlights of that missionary campaign in Ephesus are known.

After a preliminary start in the local synagogue, Paul moved his preaching and teaching to the auditorium which was also used by the Greek philosopher Tyrannus. Acts records also that Paul carried on a missionary campaign on a house-to-house basis.[3]

The story of the riot in the theatre told in Acts 19:23-41 ought to be read, not only as a piece of dramatic reporting, but also as insight into the kind of opposition likely to be stirred up by the evangelistic methods of Paul and his companions. Hitherto, opposition to Paul had been organ-

ized by the Jewish communities in the cities which he
had visited and by Jewish Christians who believed that
he was undermining the uniqueness of Judaism as the
vehicle of God's revelation. Here in Ephesus, the opposition to Paul came from tradesmen who felt that business
in the production of souvenirs was being threatened by
Paul's insistence on the unique character of God's revelation of himself through Jesus. While the account which
Luke gives will stand on its own as a piece of vivid
reporting, it is worthwhile adding some details which
Luke assumed his readers to know. For example, the
theatre at Ephesus would hold twenty-five thousand
people and was commonly used as a place for holding
"town meetings," gatherings of business men, or the kind
of meeting which might come under the heading of what
we would call "conventions."

Every large shrine in the ancient world had its own
shops and stores selling souvenirs. This is not unknown
altogether to us, although on another level. As you travel
round the country, there are to be found, at practically
every stopping place, either counters or whole stores selling "souvenirs." The similarity of the products offered
wherever you go almost leads you to suspect that there is
one massive factory producing them—with names to be
added or stamped on at individual localities! While it is
probable that many of the "souvenirs" or "devotional objects" offered for sale in the pagan shrines in the ancient
world were copied from each other, it is certain that they
were "big business."

In any event, Paul's campaign in Ephesus represented
a very real threat to the sellers of these devotional objects.
Concerned for business reputation and profits, the sellers
congregated in the theatre to hold a protest meeting and
the near riot which took place there does not read like
a convention of business men whose affairs were being
threatened by an outsider. Still, the effect which Paul

had on the local economy can be gauged by the intervention of the chief legal officer for the community (the town clerk), who succeeded in persuading the angry participants in the meeting that redress could be obtained from the courts rather than from this kind of noisy protest.

There were other sensitive matters at stake in this disturbance. The temple officials in Ephesus were responsible not only for the worship of Artemis but, at this time also, for the official imperial cult of Rome and the emperor. It was possible that they were—to use a modern phrase—"treading on eggshells." To allow an uproar because the cult of Artemis was being threatened by Paul might just possibly have led to a counter charge that a too heavy emphasis on Artemis could be interpreted as an insult to the imperial cult of Rome and Caesar! In any event, the Asiarchs (representative members of the major cities of the province) persuaded Paul not to go to the theatre. The Asiarchs were undoubtedly conscious of their own position over against that of the imperial capital of Rome and any major disturbance in Ephesus itself would almost certainly have brought down upon them some kind of official rebuke—if nothing worse—from Rome itself.

There are two other matters mentioned by Luke to which, conveniently, we may pay attention here. First, the town clerk of Ephesus referred to "the sacred stone which fell from the sky," the goddess Artemis having been originally represented as a meteorite which had fallen from the sky. Incidentally, we may recall that one sacred object still venerated by Islam is, in fact, a meteorite standing in the city of Mecca.

Second, Luke refers to a public burning of books on the part of some of the converts who had been practicing the astrological arts. It is always difficult to be happy about book burnings of any kind. Enthusiastic converts have very often destroyed, in their enthusiasm, heritages from their own past. There was, for example, the burning of the priceless library at Alexandria by enthusiastic Christians—a circumstance later blamed on Islam. The period of the Reformation in Europe saw another holocaust of priceless medieval works, and there have been book burnings of various kinds as a symbol of rejection of hated objects even in our own times. Ephesus, at the time of Paul, was undoubtedly one of the major centers of the magical arts of astrology in the Mediterranean world. Attention has been called already to the important part which astrology and similar magical arts played in the civilization of Hellenism in the Roman period. It is not that these magical practices were either Roman or Greek in origin—their origins go back to Babylonian times. But, without any doubt, the atmosphere at the beginning of the Christian era was one of ever-darkening fear. The astrologer grew rich and fat by preying on the fears of a world which was growing more and more uncertain about the direction things were taking. There was also growing up a whole realm of material which later came to be called "gnosticism," to which attention was called earlier in this book. At a later stage in Christian history, this phenomenon caused considerable anxiety to Christian writers, notably Irenaeus of Lyons. We can judge best the effect which Paul's teaching and preaching had on these converts by reflecting that the value placed upon those books was something like fifty thousand workdays in his own time. The book-burning, interestingly enough, had been sparked by some exorcists who had tried to imitate Paul's own exorcisms.

Paul's missionary work of three years in Ephesus made that city a copartner with Jerusalem and Antioch as a center of Christian influence in the Hellenistic world. In the last book in the New Testament, we get an indication of the importance of Ephesus, and of its problems with heretical groups, bearing eloquent testimony to the effectiveness of Paul's work there.[4]

Paul tells us that he engaged in missionary work in Illyricum.[5] We have no record of this evangelistic enterprise apart from this mention in his letter to Rome, but it may well have taken place on his return from Ephesus to Antioch and Jerusalem. This was certainly the farthest north that Paul ever worked, except for his final journey to Rome. On leaving Ephesus, Paul took the opportunity of covering old ground among his congregations in Macedonia and Greece. The last city he visited was Philippi. Judging by the tone of the letter to Philippi which survives in the New Testament, his converts in that city gave him far less trouble than any other group of his converts. Periodically, we are told that the Philippians represented Paul's favorite group of converts. It is hard to know upon what basis such a judgment is made, unless it is that his letter to the Philippians contains no account of any problems in that city!

After the visit to Philippi, Paul returned to Asia, leaving the ship at Troas where he stayed for a week. Luke gives an account of Paul's spending one whole night in teaching in Troas and a brief mention of his paying short visits to Mytilene, Chios, and Samos. Presumably, the Christians in these three places were people who had embraced the gospel in Ephesus, inasmuch as these three islands were all in close touch with the provincial capital of Ephesus.

Mytilene was the chief city of the island of Lesbos and had considerable reputation as a resort area. Chios was the chief city on the island of that name. As for Samos, we learn from I Maccabees that there were Jewish colonists there as early as the second century B.C.

Paul was anxious to return to Jerusalem, and so did not visit Ephesus again but arranged for the presbyters of Ephesus to meet him at the Port of Miletus. This was an important commercial city but lacked the religious significance of Ephesus. Miletus is known to us as the birthplace of famous scientists and philosophers of the ancient world. Here, for example, were born Phales, one of the greatest scholars of Greece, and Anaximander, one of the great map makers of the ancient world.

We have a very moving account of the farewell of Paul to his Ephesian presbyters. He seems to have been aware that his missionary enterprises were coming to an end and that, if he was to fulfil his vocation, it would not be possible to visit Ephesus again. Paul then sailed to Cos.

A considerable part of the population of Cos consisted of Jewish bankers, its location putting it in a strategic position to engage in the banking associated with commerce. From Cos, Paul sailed to Rhodes—a natural trading center and favorite resort area. Paul's final island stop was at Patara, the seaport of Lycia and the ordinary departure point for ships sailing to Syria, Palestine, or Egypt. The ship in which Paul was traveling reached Tyre after a journey of some four to five hundred miles. There Paul stayed for a week, after which he sailed on to Ptolemais and thence to Caesarea, which in his time was the seaport for Jerusalem.

It was in Caesarea, while Paul was staying in the home of Philip the evangelist, that Luke records the visit of a prophet called Agabus who had come from Judea. Agabus was convinced that any visit on the part of Paul to Jerusalem would end inevitably in his imprisonment and his being handed over to the pagan authorities. Luke records attempts on the part of Paul's companions to persuade him not to go to Jerusalem. Paul, however, was determined that, whatever the risks, it was to Jerusalem he must go to complete this third journey, and his parties went on to Jerusalem—about sixty-five miles away. It has been reckoned that on his third missionary journey Paul had accomplished around 2,800 miles of travel.[6]

NOTES

1. Or Diana.
2. The discovery of the temple of Artemis in the 19th century was made after patient search. Archeological work at Ephesus has continued up to the present time with remarkable success.
3. Acts 20:20.
4. Revelation 1-3.
5. Romans 15:19.
6. Unless we are to take I Corinthians 15:32 as referring to imprisonment at Ephesus, we are wholly without information as to whether or not the "captivity" letters (Philemon, Colossians, Ephesians) were written from Rome or—as some scholars have thought—from an imprisonment at Ephesus during Missionary Journey III (A.D. 54-57). Acts says nothing about such an imprisonment and, short of some new and dramatic discovery, we are unlikely to arrive at any certainty in this matter.

18.   WITNESS FOR CHRISTIANITY

(Acts 21:17 — 26:32)

PAUL WAS in Jerusalem in the year A.D. 58 to meet with James, head of the Church of Jerusalem, and the presbyters of the Church. It was obvious, in the light of the disturbances which had accompanied Paul's missionary efforts in the Mediterranean, that it was necessary for something to be done to allay the suspicions—however ill-founded—that he was seeking to overthrow the law of Moses for Jews. It was at the suggestion of James and the presbyters that Paul accompanied to the temple four men who were under a solemn religious vow, to conclude with them the final ceremonial of that vow.[1] Unfortunately, because Paul had been seen in Jerusalem in company with Gentiles, Jews from Asia created a major disturbance by shouting out that Paul had brought Gentiles into the inner courts of the temple.

Roman authorities were always sensitive to any kind of disturbance which might lead to a riot in Jerusalem and the military tribune heard about the disturbance very quickly and came down to the temple area.[2] By the time he arrived, the temple authorities had thrown out Paul and his companions and had closed the gates of the temple because they feared that the temple had been profaned by the reported presence of Gentiles in the inner courts.

The Roman commanding officer, Claudius Lysias, with a large detachment of troops, rescued Paul. Paul asked for permission to address the mob and, somewhat surprisingly, the military commander allowed him to do so. From the steps of the fortress Paul addressed the shrieking mob in Hebrew. This had the effect of producing temporary quiet.[3] Unfortunately, he laid himself open to misunderstanding by mentioning Gentiles and the mob threatened further violence against Paul. Not too surprisingly for those times, the commanding officer was about to have Paul flogged so as to subject him to questioning. At this point, that Paul claimed one of the privileges of his Roman citizenship by reminding the commanding officer that it was illegal to flog a Roman citizen. In Chapter 22 we glimpse something of the immense power which the phrase, "I am a Roman citizen," conveyed to civil and military authorities all over the Mediterranean world.

The bewilderment of the Roman commanding officer is very clearly demonstrated in Acts, and—apart from any questions of the Roman law and citizenship involved— the military tribune had to have some kind of information upon which to base a report to his superior officers. He, therefore, called together the chief priests and members of the Sanhedrin and brought Paul before them. It is possible to see in Luke's description of this appearance an attempt on Paul's part to divide the members of the

Jewish council by appealing to their theological rivalries. This may be so, and, perhaps, Paul knew enough about the constituent membership of the council to be able to identify members who were either Sadducees or Pharisees and appealed to the one question of theological debate which he knew would divide seriously his accusers. This does not seem to be entirely in line with what we know of Paul's character, but it could have been so. At any rate, Paul's principal article of defense to his accusers was what was being called in question in his own teaching —the matter of resurrection from the dead. It is certain that this was calculated to bring to the surface all the most violent hostilities of Pharisees and Sadducees toward each other, and this is what, in fact, happened. The military commander, terrified that he was about to lose his prisoner once more by mob violence, ordered his soldiers to take Paul to the barracks.

Luke then says that Paul was told in a vision that night that he would shortly be required to give evidence in Rome as well as in Jerusalem. Perhaps this is Luke's way of telling us that Paul was becoming increasingly more aware that he must now make use of his Roman citizenship to give witness to the gospel at the very center of the Roman Empire. In the meantime, some forty Jews—according to Luke—had taken a vow not to eat or drink until they had killed Paul. They had hit upon the idea of requesting a further meeting of the council for an examination of Paul, planning that they would kidnap him on the way and kill him. The news became known to Paul's nephew—an interesting sidelight on the existence of Paul's family in Jerusalem, evidently a family of some importance for the news to have reached them. The military tribune's reaction to this plot was to call two centurions and order a band of two hundred soldiers with cavalry and escort to take Paul to Caesarea and bring him before Felix, the governor.

The soldiers escorted Paul overnight to Antipatris, and the next day took him to Caesarea and delivered the report of the military tribune to the governor. The immediate decision of the governor was to have Paul guarded in Herod's headquarters until his accusers arrived.

In common with all of the cities built by Herod in Palestine, Caesarea was built in a style similar to all other Hellenistic cities with facilities for administration, sports, and all of the functions associated in those days with city life. Herod built Caesarea to be the capital of his own kingdom and to act as an outlet to the sea for Samaria. It was, for the Romans, the capital of Palestine and the chief seat of the Roman procurator. Perhaps Herod's greatest contribution to the city was the building of an artificial harbor consisting of a large semicircular wall built out into deep water with the entrance toward the north. There were, apparently, large warehouses and a roadway along the harbor wall.

In every respect, Caesarea was an important city. The reader may be interested to look back in Acts to chapter 12 for the account which Luke gives of the last dramatic appearance of Herod Agrippa before his people. There was in Caesarea a large amphitheatre which was reputed to hold about twenty thousand people and it was here that Titus, the Roman who captured Jerusalem in A.D. 70, celebrated a family occasion with over two thousand of his prisoners fighting wild animals. Altogether, Caesarea had a turbulent life. It was a particularly violent riot in Caesarea which partly precipitated the Jewish war against Rome (A.D. 66-70) which ended ultimately in the destruction of the temple. Caesarea was the home of Philip the Evangelist; it was also the place where Cornelius had been converted to the gospel. It was from here that Paul had sailed to his own home in Tarsus after his first visit to Jerusalem and it was here that he landed at the end of both his second and third missionary journeys.

The procurator, Felix (his full name was Antonius Felix), was the chief Roman official in Judaea from A.D. 52 to about A.D. 60. Pontius Pilate, who is well known to all of us, had been procurator until A.D. 36 and, although there had been five other Roman administrators between Pilate and Felix, it is Felix who is singled out by the Jewish historian Josephus as a corrupt and violently cruel administrator.[4] The wife of Felix, who is mentioned in Acts, was Drusilla, the youngest daughter of Herod Agrippa.

When Paul appeared before Felix, it is apparent that the first instinct of the procurator was to release the Apostle for lack of evidence. Then comes an interesting sidelight into the character of Felix. Paul was kept under house arrest, with considerable liberties allowed him, largely in the hope that Paul could summon up sufficient money to pay the procurator a large enough bribe to secure his release. It seems incredible that Paul's house arrest lasted under these terms for two years. Of course, this does raise the entire matter of Paul's own financial resources. Not only was Paul living under house arrest at his own expense, but also he was plainly in a position to afford the very expensive process of an appeal to the emperor. Luke tells us in Acts that Paul lived at his own expense during his entire stay in Rome and was able to afford a great amount of assistance. Paul boasted, on several occasions, in his letters that he was not ashamed to earn his own living and refused to become a financial burden to his congregations of converts. We can only speculate about the sources of Paul's relatively well-off financial status, and such speculation may conclude that Paul's own family was underwriting a fairly large amount of his financial burden.

For two years, then, Paul remained under house arrest at Caesarea. Felix was, at the end of that time, called back to Rome to answer for his misdeeds in Palestine and was replaced by Porcius Festus, who, incidentally, occupied the office of procurator for only a very short time. Paul's enemies had not given up the attempt to assassinate him and made one last attempt to have him brought back to Jerusalem for trial. The new procurator was anxious to go as far as he could in accommodating the Jews and asked Paul if he was prepared to go to Jerusalem to stand trial before the procurator there rather than in Caesarea. By this time, you can imagine that Paul had had more than enough of the kind of treatment which, in our modern idiom, we might best describe as a "run-around." He, therefore, asserted that the procurator knew that there was no substance to the charges brought against him and, if charges were to be made at all, as a Roman citizen he would appeal to the emperor. Under Roman law the procurator was bound to allow the appeal to the emperor by a Roman citizen and decided to do so.

A few days after the appearance of Paul before Festus, King Agrippa II, accompanied by his sister Bernice, came to Caesarea on a courtesy call to the new procurator. Although a Jew, Agrippa had been educated in Rome and was well acquainted with Roman ways and with Roman law. Festus turned to him for advice on how to handle Paul's case. Since he had appealed to Rome, this proceeding was quite illegal, but Paul was prepared to overlook the illegality in the interests of proclaiming the gospel to Agrippa. The account given by Luke in Acts is interesting in that it gives the reaction of a Roman administrator to Paul's proclamation of the gospel—Festus concluded that Paul was mad.

Agrippa's reception of Paul's message was one that might have been expected from a man who was living in incest with his own sister. Nevertheless, both Agrippa and Festus agreed that there was no way in which serious charges—especially capital charges—could be laid against Paul with any hope of success. It is clear that, under

Roman law, Festus could have released Paul, although the apostle had entered his appeal to the emperor. This, however, would have been, politically, a very unpopular move on the part of an administrator who had only recently entered upon his term of office. So, the decision was made—Paul's appeal to Caesar would have to stand.

NOTES

1. See footnote 4, Chapter XVI.
2. Just north of the temple, Herod the Great built a fortress for the defense of the temple area and also as a kind of precinct station to handle the great crowds in the courtyards. It is small wonder that the Roman military authorities were sensitive to any possibility of riot in the temple area because, not long before Paul's visit to Jerusalem, there had been a mob riot led by an Egyptian Jew and the Roman garrison was on the lookout for any recurrence of trouble from the same quarter.
3. It is interesting to note that it was during the course of this address that Paul used the ancient Messianic title "the Righteous One."
4. *The Works of Flavius Josephus*, Book XX, Chapters VII and VIII.

(Acts 27, 28)
19. ALL ROADS LEAD TO ROME

THE ACCOUNT of Paul's journey to Rome as a prisoner is sufficiently detailed and dramatic in Luke's Acts of the Apostles to make any attempt at a summarized narrative unnecessary. Paul's journey as prisoner took place in A.D. 60-61 and the military unit which took care of Paul and his fellow prisoners was stationed in Syria.

In order to read the account intelligently, it is necessary to recall how primitive, in our view, the Mediterranean sailing ships of the period were. This was so much the case, that journeys across the Mediterranean in the autumn were an extremely perilous undertaking. Most people whose business was not urgent chose either to travel over land or to spend the winter in some port and take up the journey later in the spring. Ships which carried cargo and a small number of passengers had one single main mast which carried a huge square sail secured to the hull by ropes at each corner. Unlike the sailing ships which belonged to the period nearer our own time, there were no smaller sails to take the force of the wind in varying directions, nor was the rigging of the ship such that the strain imparted by a very large sail on a single mast could prevent enormous pressures being exerted on the center of the hull of the ship. There was only one large steering oar, and it—together with the square sail construction—made it impossible for a ship caught in a storm to do anything other than run before the wind. We must bear all this in mind as we contemplate Paul embarking on the first leg of his journey from Adramyttium on a ship whose home port was fifty miles east of Troas. After a short stop at Sidon, the ship sailed around the eastern end of Cyprus, along the coast of Cilicia, Pamphylia, and Lycia. It was in Lycia that they stopped at Myra in the hope of picking up a grain ship sailing for Rome. Here, Paul and the other prisoners were transferred to the grain ship for the run to Rome. From Myra, the ship started west toward Cnidus, but ran into contrary winds and had to make a very long detour southwest to Crete where, at any rate, the mountains would provide some shelter against the wind.

By now, Paul was full of apprehension as to the prospects in store if the captain of the ship and the military commander were determined to try to sail for Rome in the winter. At this point read Luke's account in Acts 27 as precisely as possible. The captain of the ship was determined to take a chance with the winter winds and hoped to reach a Cretan harbor and winter there. In any event, the ship left early in October in a south wind but was very soon caught by a northeasterly gale coming off the mountains of Crete. In consequence, they had to run before the wind and pass the island of Cauda about twenty-five miles away. The storm did not abate and there was serious danger of shipwreck—an experience not unknown to Paul.[1] All the measures taken to save the ship and its cargo were to no avail—the gale did not abate its force, both sun and stars were invisible—and for two weeks the ship was driven westward across the Mediterranean. At midnight on the fourteenth day, the sailors realized that they were nearing land and hoped to save the ship by beaching it. Their efforts proved futile and the ship ran into a rock shoal on the island of Malta and began to break up.

Malta is well known to any with knowledge of World War II as a small island which stood up successfully to ferocious air attacks and as an extremely important naval base for Mediterranean operations in that same war. At the time of Paul's shipwreck, the island belonged to Rome. It was famous then, and for many years later, as a very important seaport for vessels trading with the capital city.

Paul's party was shipwrecked in October or November but was on its way again by the end of February. Since we are told that the ship carried two hundred and seventy-six persons, it was, presumably, a grain ship wishing to make an early profit on the grain trade before the spring season had really gotten under way. The new ship sailed north to Sicily to put in at the city of Syracuse, the Roman capital of the island—an island which had seen conquerors come and go and which had been at the mercy of every imperial power with ambitions. Syracuse had been in the possession of the sea people, then the Phoenicians, the Greeks, and finally the Romans. From Syracuse, the ship with Paul on it sailed to Rhegium at the tip of Italy and put in at Puteoli. This was an extremely important city from the point of view both of trade and of industry. It is not surprising that Paul found a group of Christian converts already in existence in Puteoli and he and his friends stayed with them for a week.

The Christian congregation in Rome had already been warned of Paul's arrival and a representative group was out to meet him. Paul was now in the city which was the heart and center of the Roman empire.

Enough has been written, and enough can be read, of the magnificence of the city of Rome in the time of Paul to make any attempt at an adequate description impossible in a book of this size. The reader is advised to read for himself the very clear account of Rome in the time of St. Paul in H. V. Morton's *In the Steps of St. Paul.*

When he arrived in Rome, Paul was placed under a privileged "house arrest" and was allowed a great deal of freedom to visit friends, receive guests, conduct his own correspondence, and the like. We may presume that this was due partly to favorable reports coming from Caesarea about the apostle himself and partly to the very tenuous nature of the charges against him.

The Acts of the Apostles ends much too abruptly from our point of view and we have no knowledge of Paul's trial or, indeed, of any legal proceedings in Rome against him. We must, therefore, conjecture about the possible course of events. It is likely, for example, that the reports of preliminary hearings were lost in the shipwreck. Undoubtedly there were interminable delays which frequently accompanied cases which had been appealed to the emperor. Also, it is extremely unlikely that the Jerusalem authorities ever appeared in Rome to present their charges against Paul. There is another factor to be taken into consideration here: appeals to the emperor were only made in cases involving criminal offenses against the Roman imperial authority, and it is very difficult to discover from the account in Acts precisely what charges could have been brought against Paul under this kind of heading. Another fact to be considered is that penalties for pressing false charges were extremely severe. And, to complicate the story further, we know that Festus had died during the time of Paul's arrest.

Since the emperor Nero is known to have delegated a very considerable part of Roman appeals to subordinates, if Paul was tried at all it is possible that the case was heard by delegated authority. We must suppose—in the absence of any other record—that Paul was acquitted in default of any charges being pressed against him.

Further substance is given to the above by the fact that Paul summoned Jewish leaders in Rome to his house to give his own story and it is evident that no word had reached the Jewish community in Rome of the charges against Paul in Jerusalem. They do seem to have been quite well informed about this sect on the fringes of Judaism which was called Christianity and members of the Jewish community were anxious to hear its story from Paul himself. Any possibility of violent opposition, or mob outrage against Paul, was ruled out by the protected character of Paul's residence as a Roman citizen awaiting trial.

We know that Paul used his two years in Rome not only as an opportunity for evangelization and teaching but also as a time for tidying up the administrative affairs of Christian congregations which he had founded. It was while he was in Rome that he sent a personal letter to Philemon about a runaway slave whom Paul had converted to the Christian faith. Traditionally, it was in Rome that Paul wrote what are called the "captivity letters." These are the letters to Ephesus, Philippi, and Colossae. Whatever doubts there may be about the authorship of the letter to Ephesus as being genuinely from the hand of Paul, there is grave doubt as to whether these letters were written from Rome or whether they do not, rather, belong to an earlier imprisonment—probably in Ephesus.

For the concluding years of Paul's life we are dependent entirely for information upon the shorter letters, generally called the "pastoral epistles." These are I and II Timothy and the letter to Titus. Unhappily, among New Testament scholars the genuineness of these letters is still a hotly-disputed question and it is unwise to place too heavy a reliance upon them as final authority for the way in which the concluding years of Paul's ministry were spent. For the sake of convenience and with some conjecture, however, I am going to piece together the story of Paul's final years from the hints in the pastoral letters without making any judgment as to whether the whole of those letters as they now stand are substantially from the hands of Paul.

The story of Paul's final years, then, may be summarized as follows: in I Timothy 1:3, we read of Paul's plans to go to Macedonia, while II Timothy 4:20 tells us that Paul was at Miletus and chapter 4:13 in the same letter tells us that he had also been to Troas. The letter to Titus discloses that Paul worked for some time on the island of Crete and left Titus there as his delegate.

It is in II Timothy that Paul tells of a new and quite serious crisis in his affairs. In that letter, he represents himself as having been taken to Rome as a common prisoner, without privileges, and evidently under serious charges. He speaks of one appearance in court where, he asserts, he stood completely alone. We can only guess that the charges must have been so serious that—for the sake of the work in which they were engaged—none of Paul's companions wished to be involved in the case. The letter tells us that, for all his sufferings and imminent execution, Paul was still concerned about the fate of his Gentile Christians. With the end in view, Crescens was sent to the churches in Galatia and Tychicus went on a

similar errand to the church in Ephesus. Titus himself
went to the Dalmatian coast of what is now Yugoslavia.
The apostle was filled with distress at this time by the
desertion of some of his fellow workers including some
in Ephesus who had spent so much time with him. It is
in this same letter that Paul requests Timothy to come
to him before the winter, bringing Mark with him and
records that Luke was with him. If this last reference
is genuine, then it is even more surprising that Luke did
not finish the story of Paul beyond the present ending
of the Acts of the Apostles.

Church tradition has it that Paul was beheaded just
outside the city of Rome either late in A.D. 67 or early
in A.D. 68. Church tradition also has it that it was in
the same year that the apostle Peter suffered death by
crucifixion, also in Rome.

It is difficult to know how to conclude a book largely
concerned with the apostle Paul. There has been nobody
quite like him since in Christian history and, in spite of
the fact that Paul's letters were only letters and not
formal theological documents, it is to Paul that Christian
theologians turn instinctively when the message of the
gospel must be interpreted or restated. Misunderstood,
wrongly understood, misread, or rightly interpreted, rightly understood, and faithfully studied, the influence of
Paul on Christian thinking and theological debate towers
over the Christian scene from his own day to this in a
fashion which is true of no other writer in the New Testament. Faithful Jew, internationalist, traveler, Pharisee,
and, later, the man who gave his whole life in allegiance
to Jesus as promised Messiah and redeemer, there are
facets to Paul's character, to his ministry, and to his
teaching that are always new and seemingly inexhaustible.
Plainly, he was a passionate man and a man who could
evoke passionate response whether of loyalty or of dislike.
We may be grateful that this passionate man felt so deeply

and so lovingly about his commitment of faith to God, to Jesus as the deliverer anointed by God, and to the Holy Spirit who perpetuates in the Church God's redeeming work that he left us an imperishable memorial of theological utterances which very easily slide over into hymns of praise.

NOTES

1. II Corinthians 11:25.

Appendix

CHRONOLOGY OF PAUL'S LIFE AND MINISTRY

33　Death of Stephen.
　　Conversion of Paul—working back from the "three years" of Galatians 1:18 (=Acts 9:26-29) and the "fourteen years" of Galatians 2:1 (=Acts 15:3-12) fits well with a visit to Jerusalem in 49.
　　Paul in "Arabia" (Transjordan territory).
　　"Three years" in Damascus—Acts 9:23.

40　Paul leaves Damascus (II Corinthians 11:32) and goes to Jerusalem (Acts 9:26; Galatians 1:18) to confer with Peter. Plot against him causes him to leave.

40-44　Paul in Tarsus (Acts 9:20), Syria, and Cilicia (Galatians 1:21-22). The vision of II Corinthians 12:2-4(?). Visit from Barnabas; Paul returns to Antioch.

44-45　In Antioch. Prophecy of famine (Acts 11:28).

46　Collection in Antioch for famine victims (Acts 11:29-30) is taken by Paul to Jerusalem according to Luke. Paul, however, makes no mention of a "famine" visit in Galations. Was it a separate visit from the others (*e.g.*, the visit to Jerusalem in Acts 15)? Perhaps, Luke's sources had multiple references to visits by Paul and he understood them all as separate whereas, in reality, some references might have been made to one historic occasion (*e.g.*, Acts 11:29-30; 12:25; 15:3). If this "famine" visit took place, it was very short and Paul returned to Antioch.

First Mission

46-49   Very brief account in Acts 13:3-14:26. Paul, Mark, and Barnabas go to Cyprus, thence from Salamis to Paphos and then to Perga in Pamphylia on the south coast of Asia Minor. Mark leaves the party and returns to Jerusalem. Paul and Barnabas go on to the towns of south Galatia—Pisidian Antioch, Iconium, Lystra, and Derbe. They retrace their steps and sail from Attalia for Antioch.

49   The visit to Jerusalem precipitated by a decision in the congregation at Antioch sending Paul, Barnabas, and others (Galatians 2:1) to consult with the apostles and elders about the status of Gentile converts. Were they to be circumcised and keep the Mosaic Law? Galatians 2:1 and also Acts 15:13-29 give the impression that circumcision was the *only* issue decided at this meeting. Converted Pharisees demanded that Gentile converts be circumcised *and* adhere to the Law, but the "men of reputation" (Galatians 2:2) agreed with Peter not to accede to the demand. In Paul's view, this agreement freed the Church from being bound permanently to Judaism (Galatians 2:6).

49   Peter's visit to Antioch, where first of all he shares table-fellowship with Gentile Christians and then separates himself from them when Jewish Christians arrive from Jerusalem (Galatians 2:11-13), behavior which leads to a vehement protest by Paul. We don't know what happened later, but assume that soon afterward Paul departed on his second mission. Paul never refers (see next section) in Galatians to a letter from James on the application of the food laws of Judaism to his Gentile converts. He apparently first learned of such a letter when he returned to Jerusalem in 58 (Acts 21:25).

49(?) Letter from James in Jerusalem on the dietary laws (Acts 15:13-39). Peter's behavior at Antioch, and Paul's opposition to him, didn't solve any problems there and messengers were sent to Jerusalem to ask how Gentiles were to apply the Mosaic Law, if at all. The results of the conference between James and the others were circulated in a letter to Antioch, Syria, and Cilicia. Here are the problems in Acts 15:

1. The chapter is a patchwork and the first two verses are an attempt to join two strands of sources. Verse 34 is not in the best manuscripts and must be omitted. But, if we do this, Silas is a problem. When did he join Paul on the Second Mission?

2. Who is the Simeon in verse 14? Often, he is identified with Simon Peter, but Peter is never called Simeon in the New Testament except in 2 Peter 1:1 and even there the textual evidence is indecisive. Perhaps, this Simeon is the same as Simeon Niger of Acts 13:1, sent to consult James and the Jerusalem community about the food laws.

3. Peter's address in verses 7-11 deals with circumcision, whereas James' summary of the meeting (verses 13-21) deals with the food laws and unlawful sexual practices.

We would appear to have in Acts 15 a composite of two separate events—a "council" handling the matter of receiving Gentile converts and an "encyclical" having to do with the application of the Mosaic dietary laws.

Second Mission

49-52 Paul refuses to have Mark with him as his companion because of his previous experience of Mark's leaving him. Instead, Paul takes Silas. From Antioch, through Syria and Cilicia to southern Galatia again. Takes Timothy as a companion (Acts 16:1-3). Then through Phrygia to northern Galatia to found new communities. Prevented from going to Bithynia, Paul goes to

Mysia and Troas. The "we" sections of Acts begin here at 16:10-17. In response to a dream or vision, Paul goes to Neapolis, the port of Philippi. Imprisonment for exorcising a slave girl, after which Paul goes to Thessalonica. Controversy with Jews, flight to Beroea, and then to Athens (Acts 17). Paul moves to Corinth and stays with Jews expelled from Rome by imperial edict. Stays in Corinth eighteen months.

51 *Letters to Thessalonica.*
Paul's opponents take him to the court of the proconsul who dismisses the case. Departure for Ephesus, thence to Caesarea Maritima. Visit to Jerusalem and then to Antioch for over a year (maybe fall of 52 to early 54).

Third Mission

54-57 Paul goes through northern Galatia once again to Ephesus. Stays there for three years.

54(?) *Letter to Galatia.* (Some scholars feel this letter could have been written as early as 49[?].)

56(?) *Letter to Philippi,* apparently written during an imprisonment in Ephesus. (Some scholars feel this letter could have been written as late as 62-63[?].)

57 In the spring, information reaches Paul about troubles in the church in Corinth. Four letters were sent to Corinth, of which only two are in our New Testament and one of them, II Corinthians, may be a composite. There was one letter written before our present I Corinthians (*cf.* I Corinthians 5:9). Situation sends Paul on a hurried visit to Corinth (II Corinthians 12:14; 13:1-2) which accomplishes nothing, even making matters worse. Returns to Ephesus and writes a third time (II Corinthians 2:3-4,9; 7:8,12; 10:1,9). Finally sends Titus to cope with the situation. During Titus' absence, a riot of silversmiths occurs. Paul leaves for Macedonia, meeting Titus on the way and from him learns that the situation in Corinth has improved. Paul writes to Corinth a fourth time—our present II Corinthians.

57 Paul in Corinth for three months.
58 *Letter to Rome,* probably written in Corinth.
   The Gentile Christians having taken up a collection for the poor in Jerusalem, Paul determines to go to Jerusalem himself with the collection. A plot against him, as he is about to embark for Syria, makes Paul determined to go overland through Macedonia. Christians from Beroea, Thessalonica, Derbe, and Ephesus go with Paul and spend Passover in Philippi.
   Journeys by ship for Troas, overland to Assos, and then by ship to Mitylene. Sails from Chios to Samos, then to Miletus where he meets with the elders from Ephesus. Sails to Cos, Rhodes, Patara, Tyre, Ptolemais, and, finally, Caesarea Maritima. Overland to Jerusalem.
58 Paul arrested in Jerusalem on a charge of bringing Gentiles into the inner court of the Temple. Roman military tribune sends Paul to the procurator, Antonius Felix, at Caesarea Maritima.
58-60 Paul in prison. Then, on appointment of a new procurator, Porcius Festus, appeals to Rome.
60 (Autumn) Paul leaves Myra with his escort (and Luke?), but a storm carries the ship for days across the Adriatic and, eventually, it is wrecked off Malta.
61 Paul arrives in Rome.
61-63 Paul under "house arrest" but has considerable freedom of association.
   Letter to Philemon
   Letter to Colossae
   Letter to Ephesus

We don't know with any certainty what happened at the end of this period. But, if they are genuinely Pauline, the Pastoral Letters would suggest that Paul was released and visited the east again, with I Timothy and Titus being written from Macedonia in 65. II Timothy suggests that Paul was facing arrest again and almost certain death. It may be that Paul was arrested in Troas, sent to Rome, and wrote II Timothy from prison there.